Getting Off the Fence Post

Choosing How to Face Difficult Times

William P. (Buddy) Nelson

WESTBOW
PRESS®
A DIVISION OF THOMAS NELSON
& ZONDERVAN

WestBow Press books may be ordered through booksellers or by contacting:

WestBow Press
A Division of Thomas Nelson & Zondervan
1663 Liberty Drive
Bloomington, IN 47403
www.westbowpress.com
844-714-3454

ISBN: 978-1-6642-6467-0 (sc)
ISBN: 978-1-6642-6468-7 (hc)
ISBN: 978-1-6642-6466-3 (e)

Library of Congress Control Number: 2022907569

Print information available on the last page.

WestBow Press rev. date: 04/27/2022

I want to dedicate this book of devotions to my wife, Becky, who has been my stability, support, encourager, and loving friend for forty-eight years. Without her, I would be lost. God placed her in my life for the very purpose of allowing me to slow down enough to hear the still small voice of God calling me to ministry while at the same time giving me the determination to remain faithful in God's service through the years.

I dedicate this book also to my children and grandchildren for their love and presence in my life: Bill, Maddie, and Iva Nelson as well as Brook, Tommy, Brooks, and James Woodward. I am so proud of each one of them. This project began to give them the gift of my stories and a better understanding of how I became the man I am through faith and experiencing God's love and presence. It became so much more.

Contents

Acknowledgments

I want to express my sincere appreciation to Lisa Gill, church secretary, friend, assistant, and one who could keep me focused each day. Also, the entire church staff at Lakeview Baptist Church in Oxford, Alabama, where I was serving as pastor. This special church staff has been a source of support and encouragement and became the focus for many sermon illustrations during our times of laughter and joy of ministry. They additionally walked shoulder to shoulder with me as we faced the sorrow and stress brought on by the crisis of a pandemic.

I thank Danny Freeman, a friend who read and commented often about these devotions. He is a local publisher who was an encourager and guided me to find WestBow Press.

I thank all those who encouraged and supported me in this adventure, especially the church members of Lakeview. I did not plan to publish, but their words made me feel God was a part of what was happening. This alone led me to begin this process.

I thank Ella Robinson for her willingness to edit these devotions. Ella is a professional copy editor. When we asked her to assist, she was so willing. How very grateful we are to renew old friendships and have an extreme gratitude for her assistance.

I thank Mark (Lash) LeRoux for the wonderful illustration on the cover. He is a wonderful Christian, friend, minister, and artist. He was also a professional wrestler in the past. He was so very kind to take the time to assist me. If anyone desires his artistic talents as a caricature artist, you can contact him at Lashwcw@aol.com. I would recommend him highly. He also serves as the associate pastor at First Baptist Church at McClellan in Anniston, Alabama, and is the chaplain at Legacy Assisted Living in Jacksonville, Alabama. Mark has found multiple ways to serve God effectively.

Introduction

In January 2020, America began to hear about a possible coming pandemic related to COVID-19, which was discovered in China. In the following days and weeks, there were reports of the spread of this virus and the devastating effects upon the lives of individuals, communities, and churches. It became a time to learn as much as we possibly could to help, especially when one serves as a pastor of a local church. An overwhelming feeling of responsibility blended with obligation overtook me. By March 2020, it was obvious churches needed to respond to keep the congregations safe, as well as spiritually strong. We needed to be medically wise while at the same time discovering God's will during our troubling days. On March 14, I sent our church members the following communication as a beginning of educating and preparing the church, as the COVID-19 pandemic moved closer to home.

> I know this is an anxious time in our world due to the fears and anxiety over the COVID-19 infections. I was at Sam's and Wal-Mart and Winn Dixie yesterday and was amazed at how much panic was demonstrated. I receive regular updates from the Calhoun County Emergency Management Agency, which also copies the CDC's updates and recommendations. My suggestion to each of you is to think caution, not panic. Be prepared. Do not overreact. Pray. Don't spread rumors.

So this journey of faith began. In this journey we were facing, there was no way to imagine how many crossroads would be faced ahead. Many turns and twists would be our challenge to traverse. The extent of the illnesses would mount up as the unbelievable death count was reported in our world, the United States, and even in our church family. Dealing with what we were about to face was not a choice we could make. It was here. We could not avoid it. Isn't this how most crises come our way? How we dealt with this onslaught of a pandemic was totally up to us as individuals and people of faith. Choices we faced were faith or fear—spiritually strong or saddened into depression—and even who to trust when our normal world was spinning out of control.

There was also a personal choice I was to face. As a person of faith and pastor, how was I to stay mentally and spiritually heathy? A book that greatly influenced my life when I was in seminary was Dr. Wayne Oates's *When Religion Gets Sick* (West Minister John Know Press, 1970). When we moved to Louisville, Kentucky, for seminary, we discovered our next-door neighbors were Marty and Jerry Davis. Jerry was the chief psychiatric aide at Norton's Hospital. He suggested I apply for a position as a psychiatric aide. I did and was introduced to Dr. Oates. He became my professor, supervisor, and friend as I worked at Norton's Hospital for three years. One of the great insights in this book was if a minister does not take care of their own issues, their churches can become as unhealthy as they are. Of course, this is an oversimplification of Dr. Oates teachings through his book. It has been an important aspect of ministry to be as healthy mentally, emotionally, and spiritually as I could. This was a direct result of the teachings and writings of Dr. Oates.

An emotion that guided me in those early days of pandemic was to guide the church to maintain spiritual health, assist my family, and seek God's direction for all of us. In a post sent out on March 15, I said this:

> Pray for all of our churches as we assess how to provide spiritual assistance, encouragement, and God's love through this time of the COVID-19 virus. Many aspects of our lives are being altered. A person from the Alabama Health Department gave solid advice. "Prepare as if you were preparing for a hurricane to hit your community." Many are living in fear, but we as faith believers and followers of Christ need to look at this situation as a greater opportunity to trust God, strengthen our prayer life, and worry more about others than we do ourselves. Call a senior adult, a friend, a neighbor, and offer loving

encouragement. When you want factual information go to the CDC.gov web site. They are the most knowledgeable and give facts without spin. Listen to the Alabama Health Department recommendations, and listen to the National Task Force guidelines. Finally, if you are sick, or just not feeling well, or if you have a fever, or if you have been exposed to the virus, stay home. Do not risk causing someone else to become sick or potentially die. You can always contact me or the church office.

When I reflect on the initial guidelines offered to the church, what was said was a meager attempt to convey how much of a struggle it was to convey positive, encouraging words without causing excessive fear. Then on March 17, 2020, I concluded another announcement with these words:

> Remember God has a plan. Maybe he wants us to get outside the church building for a while so we will become more creative in finding new ways to maintain our fellowship, be a witness for our Savior, and minister to people. Until the next briefing, remember I love you, but God loves us all more than we can ever imagine. He and he alone will not only see us through, he will open new doors, new opportunities, and new ways to do his work. Trust *him!*
>
> "If you hold to my teaching, you are really my disciples. Then you will know the truth and the truth will set you free" (John 8:31–32 NIV).

In an unintentional way, I now see these words as the beginning of a developing urging from God to write daily devotions to help people with whom I could not see regularly. It seemed as if I were forty-seven years younger feeling a call from God. This time a *new calling.* The first attempt to write a word of encouragement in a time of crisis was on March 19, 2020. This is what was written:

> The tranquil peace of our everyday lives becomes chaotically disrupted when we have to climb down off

our fence posts and take a stand for what we believe. In moments such as these, we discover what we really believe; we discover who we really are. The hidden inner-self comes to the surface for all to see. In John 18, Pilate asked Jesus, "Are you the King of the Jews?"

We are facing isolation, fear, anxiety, confusion, and wondering when will this virus pass from us. The psalmist said it well in Psalm 80:4 (NIV). "O Lord God Almighty, how long will your anger smolder against the prayers of your people?" Don't we feel that way at times?

We are not able to come to God's house to worship and seek answers the way we wish we could in a crisis. Maybe this is our opportunity to spiritually get outside the box of our traditional way of thinking about being in the presence of God. It is not in a building that makes us spiritually faithful. It is in our hearts.

These days will test us. Will we discover who we really are as Christ followers? Will our hidden self come to the surface and show our desire to use the tools available for us to be servants and encouragers? Will we disappoint ourselves by realizing we are not servants but complainers and problem creators?

Is Jesus your King, your Lord, your Savior, your Peace? Let the light of Christ shine in our lives so we can find his Holy presence in this world. God is in charge. God walks these lonely roads with us. God can and will use these circumstances to bring about his glory in special and unimaginable ways. Look to him!

The overwhelming response from those who read the words that I wrote was encouraging. People were indeed assisted. So the next day, I wrote another word for our benefit.

Becky (my wife) and I were talking yesterday about how this COVID-19 situation has affected us. Especially the way we are not able to meet together at church. The isolation. The quietness of walking the empty spaces of the church building. I said to Becky, "I miss most of all the handshakes and hugs." I saw Ludy Cruse, a much loved and valuable member of the church, yesterday and reached out from as far away as I could to give her a document she requested from the church. It seemed so contradictory to what I have known as ministry: no handshake nor hug.

Paul said, "Recalling your tears, I long to see you, so that I may be filled with joy" (2 Timothy 1:4 NIV).

Jesus said, "And he said unto them, With desire I have desired to eat this Passover with you before I suffer" (Luke 22:15 KJV).

Paul and Jesus himself longed with a passion to be with people. I miss the handshakes and hugs. That will not change. Yet today I celebrate the tools we have to break the cycle of loneliness. Call someone today and break their loneliness. Send a text, email, or share something good from Facebook. We are in this together. Do not feel sorry for yourself; give time to think and encourage someone else. I think it was Viktor Frankl, an Austrian neurologist, who said something like "If we could get up off our couch and go out and help someone else, we could minimize the effects of depression." Today that means using the tools we have. Who needs to hear from you?

Again, the response was positive. That was when I began to see how a few words of encouragement occasionally to the church family was a way to stay in touch with the people I love. The process of developing a devotional concept, the primary revelation in my soul, was how this became a wonderful way for me, as a Christ follower, to take care of myself. It helped me stay in touch with my emotions, my sense of spirituality, and helped me grow in my own faith development. Then another thing began to happen. I started utilizing stories from my life as ways to teach and understand scripture. What a wonderful way to leave my life stories so my children could have them in the future and my grandchildren would know more about their grandfather. There was never a thought of publishing a book of devotions. If there had, I might not have been so open about my past life experiences. I most likely would have chosen not to be so vulnerable. There were then three purposes of writing: encourage the church family, keep me mentally and spiritually grounded, and preserve my life stories.

The original intent was to write during the church shutdown due to COVID. That was originally about three months. It ended up being over four hundred devotions from March 2020 until today. There is a great appreciation on my part for so many people who have constantly said these daily words of faith needed to be published. I was humbled by that kind of response. However, I kept saying I am writing for my sanity and to leave my life stories for my family. If the church and others benefit, that is God's blessing for them.

The amazing aspect of this effort was the continuing growth in the number of people reading and responding through their comments. I heard from people I had known in high school, college, seminary, and the churches where I had previously served. I heard from friends of friends I did not know. It was indeed humbling to discover how God opened a new way to minister I would not have ventured into if there had not been a crisis. God is so good in our times of crisis, especially when we try to be faithful as Christ followers.

These devotions are a result of one pastor's need to stay in touch with his own faith and trying to faithfully follow God's guidance toward reenvisioning the future of the church with a renewed faith. The real beauty discovered is how—when living through a pandemic or a crisis of any kind—God is there with a refreshed understanding of his revelation in troubled times. God's message is the perfect help all of us need in times of personal and corporate crisis.

It is my prayer readers will find the love of Christ, along with his hope, comfort, peace, love, and joy, along with a determination to stay focused on him no matter what might be happening in our lives. God walks with us even in a crisis. He is there with us on the top of mountains and is just as real in the valleys of life. Trust him!

Remember when the world is at its darkest place, God challenges his children to shine the brightest!

Hit the Truck!

A commercial on TV shows a legal broker trying to look tough in dealing with eighteen-wheeler transport companies. He stands on top of a trailer with a sledgehammer in his hand, looking mean and angry. He wants you to believe he is mean enough to take on any trucking company who might have harmed you. His voice is loud. His face is angry. Yet every time I see this commercial, I say loudly, "Hit the truck!" I say this because he takes no action. He just stands there holding the sledgehammer.

I guess what I am expressing in my emotion is this: do not just talk a good game; take action.

> As the Father has loved me, so have I loved you. Now remain in my love. If you obey my commands, you will remain in my love, just as I have obeyed my Father's commands and remain in his love. I have told you this so that my joy may be in you and that your joy may be complete.
>
> My command is this: Love each other as I have loved you. Greater love has no one than this, that he lay down his life for his friends. (John 15:9–13 NIV)

What I believe we can say about these comments from Jesus is that God has taken action and Jesus has taken action; what are we doing to take action? Action is what Jesus is asking from us.

Because God loved us so very much, he gave to us his Son (John 3:16). Action!

Because Jesus loved us so very much, he laid down his life for us (John 15:13). Action!

Because we recognize what God has done and what Jesus has done, do we stand on top of a truck looking like we believe, or do we really take action each day, at home or not, to "love each other as Jesus has loved us" (John 15:9–13 NIV)?

Confession: I have often recognized in myself that I might be holding the sledgehammer of love, but I do nothing to prove it. Where is the action?

I would like to challenge you to do four things during this time of physical distancing, which will soon become a stay-at-home order.

1. Read through the Gospel of John.
2. Take note of the places where Jesus is performing miracles to prove his divinity.
3. Take note of the places where Jesus demonstrates his humanity.
4. Take note of where our Savior challenges us to take action.

I took a course of study at seminary on the parables. When we were studying the parable of the Good Samaritan, the professor said something that has resonated in my brain ever since. "Christianity is something you do." Tell me what you believe. Talk about how many times you read the Bible through. Show me the sores on your knees from praying. But what we need to do most of all is take action. By my actions you will know what I believe. I live the way I live because Jesus has changed my life.

Hit the truck! Take action!

Holy God in heaven, you took action to reach out to us through your Son, Jesus. Open our hearts so we will take action today to demonstrate our commitment to you. Amen.

When Fear Comes to Your House

I go back to the 1960s. I was in high school, alone at home, and heard a noise in the basement. Our dog, Prissy, began barking wildly. Then suddenly she was quiet—fearfully quiet. Then another noise. This time it was clearly a door closing. With my heart racing, I grabbed a shotgun, loaded it, and like that dumb person in a horror movie, I unlocked the basement door and began walking down the stairs. I know I should have called 911. But at this time in my life, I had no idea what 911 was all about. (The 911 emergency system was established in 1968.) So there I went.

I did not see Prissy in the laundry area, where she usually stayed. I opened the door to the downstairs room, and there, chewing on a bone that I did not give her, Prissy seemed oblivious to anything else. Then the door in the garage slammed. Feeling the false sense of courage that a shotgun gives a teenager, I ran into the garage, opened the door, and stepped outside. I saw a shadow running through the backyard. *Bam! Bam! Bam!* I fired into the air as if, in my mind, I was telling whoever it was, *Do not come back to this house.* I never found out who had entered the house that night, nor did I call police. I did not sleep at all that night.

Years have passed, and now as I look back, I think, *I know fear! I know* false *courage!* But nothing about that night has ever given me comfort.

Think about the early Christians. A knock on the door may have been people ready to arrest someone. If the person said the wrong thing to someone like Saul, prior to his conversion, that person would be done for. At any moment, they could face stoning simply because someone cried, "Heresy!"

Fear is more in the forefront of our thoughts today, though not fear of a thief or a religious zealot. It is fear of a new virus that we cannot see with our eyes. It is fear of what-if, where-from, and who-is.

I find these words from scripture comforting:

> Praise be to the God and Father of our Lord Jesus Christ, the Father of compassion and the God of all comfort, who comforts us in all our troubles, so that we can comfort those in any trouble with the comfort we ourselves have received from God. For just as the sufferings of Christ flow over into our lives, so also through Christ our comfort overflows. If we are distressed, it is for your comfort and salvation; if we are comforted, it is for your comfort, which produces in you patient endurance of the same sufferings we suffer. And our hope for you is firm, because we know that just as you share in our sufferings, so also you share in our comfort. (2 Corinthians 1:3–7 NIV)

Nine times the word *comfort* is used in that passage. God gives us real comfort! It is not false courage! It is not a victory for fear! It is our salvation that brings to us comfort in our struggles only found through faith in God.

Take the above passage and write down a few sentences that describe what these words mean to you in the circumstances we face today. Send those words you write with this scripture to a friend.

God of all comfort, be with us in this day of crisis. Amen.

In the Depths of Despair

My prayers are changing. Does that statement confuse you? I have contemplated the abyss we are standing on the edge of and wondered, like David, "How long, O Lord?" (Psalm 13:1 NIV). I, too, often look for the end rather than the present. In the middle of my fears, in the midst of my grief, in the present crisis, I need to cry, "Oh Lord, how can I make a difference?" See the change?

I love the psalms. If you read all 150 of them, you will find some confusion, some repetition, some anger, and a lot of praise. You can find a psalm to fit almost every situation in life. It is said David wrote most if not all of them. If so, and I believe he did, then we have coming out of the heart of a sinner the joy of one who was certainly redeemed. This very imperfect human being found God in every challenge of life. Don't you think that's why we, sinners in need of redemption, find our hearts being touched by these words? Look at Psalm 130.

> Out of the depths I cry to you, O Lord;
> O Lord, hear my voice. Let your ears be attentive to my cry for mercy.
> If you, O Lord, kept a record of sins, O Lord, who could stand?
> But with you there is forgiveness; therefore you are feared.
> I wait for the Lord, my soul waits, and in his word I put my hope.
> My soul waits for the Lord more than watchmen wait for the morning, more than watchmen wait for the morning.
> O Israel, put your hope in the Lord, for with the Lord is unfailing love and with him is full redemption.

He himself will redeem Israel from all their sins. (Psalm 130:1–8 NIV)

Heavenly Father, bring us peace. Allow our faith to be our strength so we can focus on you. Be with those who are suffering. Be with those families who are grieving due to the loss of their loved ones. Be with those who anxiously are waiting for the results of medical testing. Be with those who are living in isolation and fear. Be with the leaders and health officials as they attempt to guide us through circumstances we have never traveled through in our lifetime.

Gracious God of all creation, allow those who have lost their jobs to find strength and assistance to see them through the darkness of the tunnel they travel. Help me to see how I may be the answer to their prayers for guidance.

We put our trust in you, oh Lord, so hear our cry from the depths of our hearts that are breaking for all we see. But most of all, dear God, open our eyes so we can see need, open our ears so we can hear truth, open our minds so we can get beyond ourselves and discover what you want us to do as your servants, and most of all, forgive us for depending on fear more than faith. Redeem America from all our sins. Amen.

When God Speaks Softly

It was the first Sunday in September 1977. I remember it because it was the first Sunday at my first pastorate following seminary. We received the news that First Baptist Church of Roanoke, Alabama, was ablaze. It was not a revival but a fire! It devastated the facility. It was the same Sunday that Don Paulson was to preach a trial sermon and to be voted on as their new pastor. Years later Don Paulson spoke about that experience. "God worked in a mighty way through this tragedy. The people of the church have been awakened by the challenge. We have renewed our commitment to missions. Our church is alive again. In the ashes we found God's presence."

In 1987 a tornado ripped through St. Roberts, Missouri. The storm demolished a church there, and I was privileged to go with a team to help rebuild. One evening, after a long day's work in the sun, we gathered for a time of reflection and devotion. The director of missions for that area was the guest speaker. He commented, "This storm which came through our community has brought revival to our community. God was certainly seen in the aftermath of the tornado."

I found myself turning to the book of Ezekiel this morning. I am reminded that although sometimes strange, Ezekiel also has a tendency to be quite inspiring. Ezekiel and the people of Israel were residents of Babylon. The exile had gone on for so long that they had become comfortable with their new life. Caution: Whenever you find your sweet spot of complacency by your own personal River Kebar, expect a storm, and in it, you will hear God speaking softly. (See Ezekiel 1:28 and 1 Kings 19:12.) It may be in Babylon, it may be in Roanoke, it may be in St. Roberts, or it may be right now, in our city, county, state, or nation.

The storm is here. Are you listening? I mean listening when God speaks softly. I assure you the soft voice of God will not be heard in the news or from any political bullies from either of the extreme divide; you will hear it when you stop long enough to listen to the voice coming from your spiritual heart of hearts when faith takes control of your life. Listen for the soft voice of God today!

Is God's soft voice urging all of us to a higher calling beyond where we have ever been before? Is God using this time to assist us in establishing new priorities that we never imagined before? Is God allowing us to see how we have put our trust and future in the wrong things up until now and he desires from us a renewal of our reliance on him in the midst of pandemic, politics, and personal crisis? If you take time to understand Ezekiel's situation and what God was asking of him, you just might believe God is up to something today. But is anyone listening to his soft voice?

Think about this today: There are no miracles if there is no crisis. Storms cause us to struggle with our faith, and the end result is a rediscovery of God. There is always hope in the stormy times in our lives because God will not, does not, and cannot leave us isolated. It is not a problem of him speaking; it is a problem of us listening. The most important issue of all is to be determined to face your storms head on and say with Paul, "I can do everything through him who gives me strength" (Philippians 4:13 NIV). "And God is able to make all grace abound to you, so that in all things at all times, having all that you need, you will abound in every good work" (2 Corinthians 9:8 NIV).

> Holy Whisperer, "Open my eyes, that I may see glimpses of truth ... Open my ears, that I may hear voices of truth ... Open my mouth" that I might speak your truth, "Spirit divine!"[1] Amen. And amen.

---

[1] "Open My Eyes, That I May See," Clara H. Scott, 1895.

StaRt/FiNish, but Watch Out foR the MiddLe

ead how Psalm 4 begins. "Answer me when I call to you, O my righteous God. Give me relief from my distress; be merciful to me and hear my prayer" (Psalm 4:1 NIV). A sweet, simple prayer each of us might offer at this time in our lives. Right? And we should pray knowing only God can give us relief.

Now read how the psalm ends.

> Many are asking, "Who can show us any good?" Let the light of your face shine upon us, oh Lord. You have filled my heart with greater joy than when their grain and new wine abound. I will lie down and sleep in peace, for you alone, oh Lord, make me dwell in safety. (Psalm 4:6–8 NIV)

See how this psalm opens our thoughts and understandings toward how to talk with God. "Hear my prayer. You alone make me dwell in safety." Great prayer for the times we live in.

I, however, cannot stop there and be faithful with God's Word. The start is David's appeal to God. The finish is David's appeal to God and assurance of God's presence. The middle is written as if it is God talking to us. Is not this how David wants this song sung in worship? This is one of the reasons I regret leaving out a stanza of a hymn. That stanza may very well tie together the entire hymn.

So what's so important about the middle of this psalm? Listen.

- "How long will you turn my glory into shame?" (Psalm 4:2 NIV)
- "How long will you love delusions?" (Psalm 4:2 NIV)
- "How long will you seek false Gods?" (Psalm 4:2 NIV)
- "The Lord will hear when I call to Him!" Psalm 4:3 NIV)

We want the relief from our distress. We want God's safety. So what are we doing to prove we are worthy of what we are asking for? Why should God listen to our prayers when we are not consistent in our daily lives? What keeps us from being secure in our faith? It is our weakness to trust in ourselves and other humans rather than depend on God alone.

Consider this. When we leap over into the grace of God truth in the life and message of Jesus, we discover that God has done, is doing, and always will do what is best for his people. He wants to demonstrate his grace of love and forgiveness every moment in every day. He may discipline us as a loving parent will do. He does so only to guide us back to the place where we can know him better. God does not love us as the world loves us. While we were sinners, Christ died for us. Scripture reminds us that "all who call on the name of the Lord will be saved" (Romans 10:13), even though we have all sinned and fallen short of God's expectations (Romans 3:23).

When we are Christ followers, we should pray with confidence and humbleness asking not for just our needs but also thanking God for what he is doing and helping us to understand why that is best for us. Constantly, we should ask for forgiveness for our failures. Yet just as constantly, we should seek God's plan in all things. May we move away from fear, anxiety, and choosing sides regarding who we think is worthy to trust. When we do embrace life with faith, confidence, and assurance of God's presence, the whole world will look completely different. We will finally see it as God's world with God's plan at work.

Today, oh Heavenly Father, you who know the beginning and the end and even the middle of life's experiences, we want to learn to trust you, for you are in control and we sincerely want to trust you. Amen.

Oh, Please Be a Policeman!

(Caution: Preacher has gone to meddling. Do not read if you are in a bad mood.)

The day I turned sixteen, my mother drove me to a place where I could demonstrate that I could drive. When I finished the driving test, I had a pink slip of paper to prove that I was legal to drive. The real license would come in the mail. What does a sixteen-year-old do after getting their first license? I said, "Can I borrow the car and go meet some friends." So here I go. We were at a Dobbs House or a Huddle House; I do not remember which. Suddenly a girl said, "Oh, no, I'm late! My parents will ground me!" Wanting to be the hero who could sweep in and save the damsel in distress, I said, "I can get you home!" So down Highway 280 we went, going south, toward her house, crossing over Lakeshore Drive, when the flashing blue light came up behind me with that awful-sounding siren. His words were "Son, did you know you were going in excess of seventy in a fifty-five-mile zone?" I said, "Yes, sir," because I did not want to admit to ninety.

Yes, I got the girl home in record time, but boy, was I in trouble.

I tell you that story to explain I was never a good driver. Now that I have years of experience behind me, I am trying to do better and be safer. When I leave my home to drive to the church, I drive down the Veterans Parkway, come over the hill, and immediately slow down to fifty where the sign is located. On many trips, there is a policeman sitting where you turn right to go to Donoho School. Almost every time I make this drive, and especially when I am being a very good driver (sense my prideful attitude), a car or two will come flying past me going at least seventy miles per hour.

I think, *Oh, please be a policeman up ahead.* There is something in the Bible about vengeance belonging to God, isn't there? (Romans 12:19 NKJ).

During this time when we are to stay at home, I hope you will take the time to process how we should act as Christians. Read through the Sermon on the Mount in Matthew 5–7. Take each part and apply it to your life. Determine how you want to be different when this isolation is all over. Maybe we should change our way of thinking. I feel it might be best, the next time someone comes flying past me, coming down the mountain on the Veterans Parkway, I should say a prayer instead of wishing a penalty on them.

> You have heard that it was said, "Love your neighbor and hate your enemy." But I tell you: Love your enemies and pray for those who persecute you, that you may be sons of your Father in heaven. He causes his sun to rise on the evil and the good, and sends rain on the righteous and the unrighteous. If you love those who love you, what reward will you get? Are not even the tax collectors doing that? And if you greet only your brothers, what are you doing more than others? Do not even pagans do that? Be perfect, therefore, as your heavenly Father is perfect. (Matthew 5:43–48 NIV)

God of grace, you have loved me even when I have not been perfect. Please keep that driver safe, and do not let them bring harm to others. Father, the next time I speed, convict me to slow down. Amen.

When It Is Worth the Sacrifice

I n any sport, you can hear coaches say, "Give 100 percent, 100 percent of the entire time, but save your very best for the final minutes." How many golf matches are lost on the last hole? How many tennis matches are lost in the last set? How many football games are won or lost based on the willingness of the players to sacrifice so much during the spring, summer, fall, and even the week of the game, that the winner is just in better physical shape in the fourth quarter than the opponent? Winning just comes easier when you are in the best possible shape.

When running a mile, one person may sprint out on the first lap, only to fade before the fourth. Winning is a matter of knowing you have what it takes to finish with your best.

Mark 14 begins with a beautiful yet tragic story just before the Last Supper Jesus would spend with his disciples. It begins with a plot by the teachers of the law and the chief priests to find a safe time to arrest Jesus. Then suddenly we are ripped away from this idea of treason to the beautiful story. Mark says, "A woman came and poured an expensive jar of perfume on Jesus" (Mark 14:3). In John's Gospel, chapter 12, we learn it was Mary, the sister of Lazarus (John 12:3). We are shocked to discover the perfume was worth a year's wage. What a beautiful expression of love, devotion, and gratitude!

You know the why of this sacrifice, don't you? Mary's brother, as said in the Gospel of John, Lazarus was present at the meal. He had been resurrected by Jesus (John 11). It was Mary saying out of the emotion of her heart, 'For all you have done for me, this is the least I can do for you. It was worth the sacrifice!'

The value of any sacrifice is the feeling of appreciation, devotion, and love one person has for the other. We can comprehend Mary's sacrifice for Jesus, though we might not be able to imagine giving anything of that value to any person we know. She recognized that Jesus made it possible for her to spend more time with her brother.

One other sacrifice begs to be discussed here. It is the giving of 100 percent by God. "For God so loved the world that he gave his one and only Son, that whoever believes in him shall not perish but have eternal life" (John 3:16 NIV). Even when we look through the Old Testament, we witness a continual lack of appreciation for all that God had done for his people. God still sent his only begotten Son, and Jesus gave his life for us. "But God demonstrates his own love for us in this: While we were still sinners, Christ died for us (Romans 5:8 NIV). Mary's sacrifice was worth it because of what Jesus did for Mary. The other sacrifice, God's only Son given to us, has yet to be proven worth the gift because God gave, trusting us to become worth the sacrifice. "Greater love has no one than this, that he lay down his life for his friends (John 15:13 NIV). "A new command I give you: Love one another. As I have loved you, so you must love one another (John 13:34 NIV). Get it? The difference between human response and divine response. Is your life worth what has been sacrificed for the *potential* God that sees in you? Are you becoming a living example that the sacrifice was worth the effort? Something to consider during any crisis. Something to consider while we are asked to sacrifice our freedom to move about. Is saving other lives worth the sacrifice made on our behalf?

Finish with your best!

Father of attitudinal change, teach us to think more of others than we do for ourselves. This and this alone teaches more about Christ's love and forgiveness than any other aspect of our faith. Amen.

What Will Be Said?

Saturday, I went out for my daily walk. I call it my daily exercise walk. It is only "daily" when I feel like getting out. It is only an exercise walk when I have something on my mind and I am trying to work it out in my head. On most Saturdays, runners and walkers come to Buckner Circle, where we lived at the time, for their real exercise and a time to be social. So on Saturdays, I walk in the opposite direction from the runners so they will not notice how slow I am. I may be older, but I am still competitive. I passed a group of about seven or eight runners with one lady a few yards in the lead. When I was coming around the circle on the backside, I met them again. This lady seemed surprised to see me at the pace I was going and said, "Good job."

I realized that it felt good for someone, who I did not know, to say, "Good job." She truly lifted my spirits by simply saying that.

Jesus is recorded in a parable in Luke 19:11–27 and in Matthew 25:14–30, with the master of a house affirming two faithful servants by saying, "Well done, thou good and faithful servant" (Luke 19:17 and Matthew 25:21). This is the story of the three servants who were given different talents or minas, while the master was away. Two were praised while the third was punished for doing nothing with his responsibility. These parables seem to imply the master of the house as being Jesus and the servants as those whom Christ has given a responsibility. Those who were faithful to multiply what master had entrusted them with were the ones who received the "Good job" or "Well done." The implications of Jesus sharing this parable is a reminder how we will be evaluated by him on the life we live here on earth when we get to heaven. We should all want him to say to us, "Good job" or "Well done." These two parables seem to be the same story remembered by the two Gospel storytellers with slight variations. The differences are not the issue. We believers should want to hear Jesus say, "Well done," when we arrive at our final destination in heaven. This is a true assumption, but does the story's message end there? I think not.

Yes, when we get to heaven, we want to hear Jesus say we lived well as his followers, but isn't it also important to believe that in whatever we do every day we can lay our head on the pillow, close our eyes, and hear Jesus say you did good today? What will be said about your life? How well have you used God's gifts entrusted to you in his service? Have you invested it in some way to be in a position for Jesus to say, "Well done," just as the master spoke to the two faithful servants at the end of each day (Luke 19:17 and Matthew 25:21)?

When we get through a crisis, what will Jesus say about our actions?

When it comes to being faithful, rather than fearful, what will Jesus say about our actions?

When it comes to praying for others, rather than being self-consumed, what will Jesus say about our actions?

When it comes to being an encourager, rather than a discourager, what will Jesus say about our actions?

When it comes to discovering truth from legitimate sources, rather than spreading rumors, what will Jesus say about our actions?

Read Luke 19:11–27 and Matthew 25:14–30. Then consider this: "Now it is required that those who have been given a trust must prove faithful" (1 Corinthians 4:2 NIV).

At the end of each day, will it be said you proved faithful today?

God, walk with us and be patient with us, until we understand your calling to do a good job every day. Amen.

Interpreting Your Past

told Becky that I needed to stop telling so many stories about me. It seems to me that if this daily devotion continues very long, I will maintain very few secrets about my life. We all live with secrets, don't we? Oh well. Here is another one.

Mother and I were traveling to Mississippi, her home state, for the memorial service of her sister. Due to the circumstances, Mother wanted to talk about her memories growing up in Mississippi. Many stories I had heard all of my life. Others were surprisingly—or should I say shockingly?—new stories I had never heard. Then she turned to me and asked if I wanted to get all of our family history background so I could tell it in the future the way she remembered it. Jokingly, I said, "No. If you do not tell me, then I can tell our history the way I want to, rather than what you want to tell me." We had a good laugh, then she went on to tell me anyway. What I remember, however, is the way I wanted to tell our history in the first place.

Is it not interesting that we like for people to hear our stories as we perceive them to be, rather than the factual circumstances as they really were? This was not the case with Paul. Read again his testimony in Acts 9. Contrast verses 1 and 15. "Meanwhile, Saul was still breathing out murderous threats against the Lord's disciples" (Acts 9:1 NIV). "But the Lord said to Ananias, 'Go! This man is my chosen instrument to carry my name before the Gentiles and their kings and before the people of Israel'" Acts 9:15 (NIV).

It would have been much easier for Paul to simply share a testimony starting with "God stopped me on the road to Damascus (Acts 9:3) and sent Ananias (Acts 9:10–16) to help me understand God had chosen me to go to the Gentiles." Now that is a great starter. However, no life-changing experience with Christ is complete without understanding the distance traveled (how far one has come) to truly know Jesus. Paul would even say, "This *is* a faithful saying, and worthy of all acceptation, that Christ Jesus came into the world to save sinners; of whom I am chief" (1 Timothy 1:15 KJV). In other words, "I am no better than anyone else. If God can save me from what I was, he surely can save you."

What is your story? How do you view the past? How has God changed you?

During this time of crisis, maybe it will be a good time to self-evaluate our Christian experience. A time of seeing through honest eyes how God has changed you and how much further you need to travel on this journey of faith. Maybe God is using this time to allow us to slow down, think, remember, evaluate, and come out on the other side of isolation a much better person and follower of Christ. Pray about it.

Holy God, help me to honestly see who I was, who I am, and who you want me to become. Amen.

Divine Challenge to Change

We have faced so many changes in our lifetime. Just think about it. When I was younger, there were 4 billion people in the world; today that number has doubled. The Iron Curtain is gone. The 1960s were filled with protests and turbulence. A US president resigned after the political scandal called Watergate. The Vietnam War ended and more wars began: Grenada, the Persian Gulf War, the invasions of Afghanistan and Iraq, and others. Now we are experiencing the effects of a pandemic on our lives. We are experiencing isolation and even having to figure out how to have "family time."

Most of what we deal with in life can be summarized by the one word we seem to hate: *change*. We long for "the good ole days" "the way things used to be." And we pout, "We have never done it this way before!" It embarrasses me every time I remember how I resisted learning how to use computers and how I said I would never use a cell phone. Now I am lost without them. Change is not always a bad thing. In most cases, we learn new things that help us in the future in ways we never imagined. Just think what today would be like if technology were not helping us stay in touch with each other and the world.

Churches resist change also. In Acts 15 we find an interesting situation. Look at "Some men came down from Judea to Antioch and were teaching the brothers: 'Unless you are circumcised, according to the custom taught by Moses, you cannot be saved.' This brought Paul and Barnabas into sharp dispute and debate with them" (Acts 15:1–2 (NIV). In my mind, I interpret this as "We have never done it this way before. You must conform to the old ways."

Another interesting fact, this one found in Acts 11:26, is that the believers were first called Christians in Antioch. Paul was doing something right. Yet here it is again, resistance to *change*. This early church conflict dealt with accepting people who are different. The result of the Jerusalem council was "Now then, why do you try to test God by putting on the necks of the disciples a yoke that neither we nor our fathers have been able to bear?" Acts 15:10 (NIV).

What concerns me most these days is how we tend to want to blame others for the problems we face. We want to blame the Chinese for the virus. We want to, depending what side we are on, blame Republicans or Democrats for our problems. We want to blame this person or that person. Do you believe in God's grace for *all* people? Do you believe *all* have sinned?

Do you believe *anyone* who calls on Jesus can be saved? (Acts 2:21 KJV and 1 Corinthians 1:2 NIV)). Do you believe "For God so loved the world" (John 3:16 NIV)?

The key word here seems to be *acceptance*. Look into the eyes of another person, whether they are divorced, are a different gender, are a different race, have a different theology, or are different in any way, and think, *God loves this person just as much as he loves me.* Let's learn to accept our situations. Learn to accept people. Learn to accept *change*. For when we do, we just might discover God at work in our world, asking us to join him in what he is doing.

> *Divine Giver of all things and all people, give us the courage to accept your divine challenge to change to become like Christ. Amen.*

How Clean Is Your House?

The stay-at-home mandate that was given to us during this crisis will save lives. It is for our safety and the safety of others. I do not disagree with this. However, it has brought to me a sense of amazement and embarrassment. While spending time at home, I have ventured where no man has ever gone before. I'm not talking about *Star Trek*. I am talking about seeing things I have not wanted to notice before. You know: out of sight, out of mind.

Let me begin with my bathroom closet. I have a habit of just putting things on the shelf without really organizing or having a plan. I realized this morning that it will take me about three hours this afternoon to empty, organize, throw away things, and then put back some of it in order where I can find what I need. And yes, I found medicine that was three or four years out of date.

Then there was the refrigerator. (Sorry, Becky.) Let me begin with my final thought before I go into detail. What was unseen should have remained unseen. We decided to really clean the fridge. I said, "I will take out the shelves, brackets and all, and really get it clean." As Becky's mother would have said, "Oh dear!" About a year ago, in my memory, I knocked over a bottle of V-8 juice. I cleaned it very well so there was no visible evidence of my clumsiness. Well, when the refrigerator was all empty, as it should have been before, there it was. The remainder! Hard, crusty, and gross. My accident was discovered. Now it is clean.

Paul talks to Timothy, a young minister, regarding some things that are of vital importance. I think it would do each of us good to read the whole chapter today (1 Timothy 4). Then look closely at these words: "Be diligent in these matters; give yourself wholly to them, so that everyone may see your progress." The key thought, though there are many others, is "So that everyone may see your progress" (1 Timothy 4:15 NIV).

All too often, we develop the idea that a person who has publicly determined to become a follower of Jesus has done all they need to do. That's like putting everything on shelves in a closet with no order or reason. Or maybe it's like cleansing them with baptismal waters without helping them empty their old ways and teaching them to start over, totally clean.

Being a believer is a process of developing one's faith (1 Corinthians 3:2). There is a starting point with no end point until we join Christ in heaven. My father had a saying that I have cherished more and more through the years. "Becoming a Christian is giving everything you know about yourself to everything you understand about God." This means at different points of our lives we need to update our beliefs based on our new understanding about ourselves and God. This is the progression of faith Paul is emphasizing.

Is your faith progressing? Can others see the progress you are making? Read 1 Timothy 4 once again, and let it sink in.

Then clean your bathroom closets and your refrigerator, but most importantly, your life.

> You love us, God, with all of our problems. May we feel so different in your presence we want to cleanse ourselves inside and outside. Amen.

Places You've Been to Discover Spiritual Solitude

Many places, locally and in foreign lands, have been special to me. Looking back, I recognize places and moments in time where my life and my faith merged just by being there. In the solitude of the moment, my life felt a special spiritual connection. The issues of the day, the challenges of the future, and the craziness of life were totally forgotten. I was at peace with myself and with God, a time when God was most real and my faith was nourished.

One such place was sitting on the western shore of the Sea of Galilee near the town of Tiberias. It was about 4 a.m. and I was waiting for the sun to rise over the Golan Heights. Sitting there alone, because the day of travel before had been exhausting and other people were sleeping the moment away, I began to remember where I was. "Some time after this, Jesus crossed to the far shore of the Sea of Galilee [that is, the Sea of Tiberias], and a great crowd of people followed him because they saw the miraculous signs he had performed on the sick. Then Jesus went up on a mountainside and sat down with his disciples" (John 6:1–3 NIV). I was sitting a few hundred yards from the place where Jesus feed the 5,000 with a meager meal of a small boy. You remember the story. Jesus was able to nourish all those who wanted to follow and hear his words (John 6:1–15).

Suddenly, the sun began to rise. In that misty moment, the sun seemed to allow me the joy of seeing its movement breaking through that early time of day. There was a chill in the air just before the warmth of the sun could reach me. Seemingly, I felt closer to God and the reality of Christ at that moment more than ever before. It was a discovery of the value of spiritual solitude! Like the masses being fed, my soul was being fed as never before.

It is interesting to me why people say they want the stay-at-home order lifted. The primary rationales seem to be money, sports, getting together with others, and getting back to the rush that stressed us out so much before. What if God is wanting us to utilize this time to discover spiritual solitude? Are we so addicted to the crazy, busy lives we have been living that we have neglected special time with God?

It was very difficult to rise at 3:30 that morning in Israel, to dress, and to walk out alone to the shore of the Sea of Galilee and wait for the sunrise. What if I had not? I am so glad I did!

Paul says, "And we know that in all things God works for the good of those who love him, who have been called according to his purpose" (Romans 8:28 NIV). Are we taking advantage of this moment to have a new discovery of spiritual solitude?

Remember the words of the hymn writer W. D. Longstaff. "Take time to be holy, speak oft with thy Lord; Abide in Him always, and feed on his word; Make friends of God's children, help those who are weak; Forgetting in nothing his blessings to seek."[2]

"Make every effort to live in peace with all men and to be holy; without holiness no one will see the Lord" (Hebrews 12:14 (NIV).

Mighty Eyeopener of our hearts, lead us to the peace and the holiness found in solitude. It is the only way to see you. When we see you, others will see you in us. Amen.

---

[2] Words by William D. Longstaff in 1882. Music by George Stebbins in 1892. Published in a variety of hymnbooks in 1892.

Be Creative; Think Like Paul

(If you feel lonely, isolated, or frustrated, call someone and break their loneliness, isolation, or frustration. Take your situation and use it to help others.)

This morning started early. I awoke with the idea in my head that I had no idea in my head. *What should I say in today's devotion?* Usually, I find myself struggling with *which* idea to follow. The emptiness of my thoughts only reiterated to me that something in my head was not working correctly. (OK, friends, enough of the quick comebacks you are thinking because of what I just said.) Then I read a passage I had marked in my Bible: 2 Corinthians 1:1–11. I will be referencing multiple passages today, but I will not this time properly quote them formally. I am using the NIV Bible. I want you to open your Bibles and read along as we proceed.

The passages referenced today are from verses 3–7, but verses 8–11 seem to explain the others so I will begin there. Paul talks about how he wants those in Corinth to be informed, aware that they—Paul and company—had been facing hardships. Their challenges were so massive and the burden so heavy that they resorted to wanting to die rather than endure more of what they were facing. Helpless! Hopeless! Through this experience of great anguish and despair, separation, and loneliness, they learned to rely on God rather than themselves. This is the reason they could boldly proclaim what Paul references in verses 3–7.

Now that we have the full picture of why Paul could say what he said, let's look back to the earlier verses. He praises God and Jesus for their compassion and comfort. Remember when Jesus said, "But the Counselor, the Holy Spirit, whom the Father will send in my name, will teach you all things and will remind you of everything I have said to you (John 14:26 NIV)"? Through the Holy Spirit we find comfort. As I will be pointing out in the message Sunday, grief will turn to joy. This is what God does for us. As Paul proclaims, having come through his personal journey of hardships, God comforts us when we are facing trouble, but not just so we can feel good. He comforts us so we can more authoritatively offer comfort to others, no matter what their hardships might be.

Thinking like Paul allows us to be creative in our approach toward life's challenges. Christ suffered for us so we might find compassion and comfort from God. Paul suffered because of Christ, so he could discover in the midst of his despair Christ's compassion and comfort. Paul then says his comfort was to encourage the Corinthians that they too can be comforted by the purity of Christ's love for them. It is through suffering we learn to appreciate all that God has done for us and can truly become his witnesses by telling a suffering world God compassionately loves them and will comfort them. We are the proof, says Paul.

In the back of my mind, I hear, "Amen," and "Preach on, brother," because all this was from the Bible and for the church at Corinth. However, we cannot leave it in the past. It is for us today as we face COVID-19 and the varied lifestyle challenges that the virus has generated. We hear the posturing and boisterous claims of politicians. We hear the warnings of the science and medical community. We hear the demands for sports, the economy, church gatherings, and on the list goes. We hear all the chatter, and we begin to pick sides and put blame wherever it might land.

Who is thinking like Paul and saying this is for our own benefit and an opportunity to be the voice of calm? Who is saying if we open our hearts and eyes and souls to God, we can find peace, comfort, and meaning? Who is saying, "Praise be to the God and Father of our Lord Jesus Christ, the Father of compassion and the God of all comfort, who comforts us in all of our troubles, so that we can comfort those in any trouble" (2 Corinthians 1:3–4 NIV)? Paul is. What say you?

Jesus, give us the heart and passion of Paul so we see others' needs more than our own. Amen.

There Is Conflict: Peace versus Fear

Caution: do Not Read if you Like things the way they are!

Peace comes with acceptance. Fear comes with change. Acceptance embraces where we are and looks for what new blessings are ahead. Fear causes us to want to return to what we called normal. Where we are is unknown. What we called normal: were we just comfortable in tolerating it or was it good for us?

I woke up this morning as usual. Made my coffee. Watched the news. Had my breakfast. Walked the dog. Then my mind kicked into gear. What do I need to do? Where do I need to be? Oh, yes, I need to write my devotion for the day. When I sat down, I heard the garbage truck. I had to get up, toss a few more things in the trash, and get the container to the road. Then I needed more coffee. I sat back down and looked at the computer. I needed to get up again and check on something else. No, I needed to answer my phone messages. I came back to the computer. Brook, our daughter, sent cute picture of James, our youngest grandchild. I had to respond. Deep breath! Now I am ready! For what? What am I doing? I am going back to the same rush of life I was in when things were "normal." This is not good. I do not like it! Have you ever felt that way?

Jesus says, "Peace I leave with you; my peace I give you. I do not give to you as the world gives. Do not let your hearts be troubled and do not be afraid" (John 14:27 NIV). A. T. Robertson in *Word Pictures of the New Testament* said, "This is Christ's bequest to His disciples before He goes …

Here and in John 16:33 (He) is using it in the sense of spiritual peace."[3] We often say in churches, "Peace be with you," as if we are saying, "Live a life of peace." But that seems to be such a contradiction in the way we live. The peace God sent into the world through his Son, Jesus, is an inner peace of the soul that cannot be understood through a lifestyle that is so busy, so hectic, and so filled with worry and fear that we cannot stop the madness to experience God's love, joy, hope, and *peace*.

I, for one, am coming to the conclusion that I do not ever want the world to be as it was before. My fear is only that we do not learn from what we are going through. We need to slow down! We needed to have time with our families, again. We need to learn all over again how much we need each other. God's peace, spiritual peace, is life without fear, for we know we are in God's hands and he alone is in control.

How do we find peace within our souls when the winds of chaos and change are raging? Maybe we find it like in Mark 4 when Jesus calms the fears of the disciples when the storm was about to wash over them. He said, "'Quiet! Be still!' Then the wind died down and it was completely calm. He said to his disciples, 'Why are you so afraid? Do you still have no faith?'" (Mark 4:39–40 NIV). Faith equals peace!

Jesus often went off to pray. He needed solitude. He needed to change the pace of life. He needed to prepare for what was ahead. He needed to reconnect with his Heavenly Father. He needed to constantly rediscover *peace* to overcome fear.

Peace be with you. Spiritual peace. Peace that leads to the enjoyment of family, life, and what God is about to do in our world today. Peace that brings calmness and enables us to slow down enough to know God.

God, give us the wisdom to do the right thing and put behind us selfish wants, especially when the right thing can save lives. Amen.

---

[3] *Word Pictures of the New Testament.* A. T. Robertson. Holman. October 1, 1958.

Negotiating with God

Have you ever been in a high-stakes negotiation? I mean a negotiation where your entire future rests upon the outcome. Not only will the outcome be life-changing for you, but the lives of many people, maybe an entire nation, will rest upon your shoulders. I met a man in 1985 while I was pastor of First Baptist Church of Oxford, Alabama. We were celebrating the 150th anniversary as a church. Former members were invited to attend, and I was told that a Dr. Robert Andrew Hingson was planning to be there. I really had no idea who this man was, yet after talking to him and researching this humble man's life, I discovered I was in the presence of greatness. Real greatness!

Dr. Hingson, among many other accomplishments, was the inventor of epidural anesthesia for childbirth and the jet inoculation gun. This gun was used to inoculate the world against smallpox. In 1958, 150,000,000 people died worldwide because of smallpox. By 1968 that number was down to about 65,000. The jet inoculation gun was used also to inoculate against influenza, cholera, typhoid, and polio. Toward the end of his career, he and his brother established the Brother's Brother Foundation in Pittsburgh. Serving God by serving the underprivileged was his calling. Yet he had an outstanding medical career and served in our nation's military.

One man from Oxford, Alabama, literally changed the world we live in today.

Early in his life, he struggled with the idea of following a call into ministry. Even his parents urged him to follow ministry. Instead, he followed what he perceived to be a call into medicine. In doing so, he did more for God's kingdom than any one minister ever could have done. You need to read his story.

In Judges 6, we read the story of the call of Gideon. Working for his father, Joash, Gideon was trying to make a living as he lived in fear, as all the Israelites did, under the rule of the Midianites. An angel, or messenger from God, came and said God had chosen him to defeat the Midianites. Then the negotiations began. Finally, Gideon agreed. In Judges 6:36–40, we read the story of "OK, God, prove yourself again." This is where Gideon tried to fleece God.

I tell you these two stories simply to say this: During this slow-down period in your life, is God calling you to do something other than what you are doing now? You might not become a Robert Hingson or a Gideon, but God is always calling his people to do things above and beyond what they think they can do themselves. We just have to listen. Are you listening? We just need to be available. Are you available? How is—I don't mean *is*; I mean *how is*—God speaking to you today? It does not matter your age, your income, or your life's circumstances. It only matters if you will make yourself available and listen!

God, tell me today how you want to use me. I will be still for a time today to listen to your angel. Tell me how I can better serve you today, tomorrow, and in the days ahead. I am yours; you are mine. I want to be involved with you or at least support those who can do more than me. Amen.

How Do You Choose to See It?

(My simple thoughts regarding truth greater than all wisdom.)

Sunday was another day of interesting thoughts. Between Sunday school and worship, a seed was planted in my heart that caused me to go home and do some studying. This is not a bad thing. It has always been my prayer that something I may say when preaching or something expressed in Bible study would create such an interest in attendees that seeds would be planted so folks would go home and do personal study. Here is what resonated with me Sunday: how are we to understand the difference between being in Christ and having Christ in you? In the Sunday school class, the thought was expressed first as "We are to be in Christ." "Those who obey his commands live in him, and he in them. And this is how we know that he lives in us: We know it by the Spirit he gave us" (1 John 3:24 NIV). See the play of wording? Maybe I make too much of this, but it fascinates my spirit: "in him"/"in us." Then the pastor preached a wonderful message in worship on Sanctification using 1 Corinthians 1. "To the church of God in Corinth, to those sanctified in Christ Jesus and called to be holy, together with all those everywhere who call on the name of our Lord Jesus Christ—their Lord and ours" (1 Corinthians 1:2 NIV). The Greek word here in verse 2 "sanctified in Christ and called to be holy" is *hagiazo*, being translated as holy, holiness, sanctification, or sanctify. It appears to be in the past tense. Something that has happened already. This brings up the challenge I faced in my own attempt to understand the reason we sometimes read "in Christ" and "Christ in us."

Maybe what scripture is saying is when we are living with "Christ in us," we are in the process of "being sanctified." The process of being changed into the likeness of Christ. If this is true, when we make a genuine determination to be a follower of God's Son, Christ lives in us as his Holy presence, to begin the molding and reshaping of our lives out of the old self to become the new person we were always intended by God to become. Step by step, Christ is creating a new person, until we become more like Jesus himself (Romans 6:4). Then if this is true, we not only have "Christ in us" but are actually "in Christ." When Christ came into the world as a baby in Bethlehem, I was taught by my father who said each year, "God wrapped Himself up in human flesh and came into our midst as a baby." We call this the incarnation. (See John 1.)

The question I ask is this: how do you choose to see it? I am talking about the idea of being "in Christ." If "Christ being in us" is the expression of being in the process of becoming like Christ (sanctification), then could we not also imagine that when we are "in Christ," we could be talking about human beings so wrapped up in the divine being that as we live, the world no longer sees us but they see Christ himself? Would that not be a great goal of everyone who follows the teachings and leadership of Christ? The world would change. They would know the true Christ by seeing him as we live our lives.

How do you choose to see it?

For further reading, look at Acts 24:24, Romans 3:24, Romans 8:1; 39, Romans 6:11, Galatians 2:20, and 1 Peter 5:10. These are some of the references to "being in Christ." Also, Acts 9:22, Romans 8:10; 12:5, Colossians 1:27, and 1 Corinthians 3:1; 15:22 for a few references regarding "Christ in you."

Ever-present challenging Father, your Word recorded in our Holy Scriptures is sometimes complicated to understand and sometimes amazing to process through. Thank you for the gift of growing closer to you through your holy guidance. Give us wisdom to understand and energy to seek your highest thoughts. Forgive us if we are not on the correct tracks of understanding, but may we always find your inspiration for today. Amen.

Open My Eyes, Open My Ears, Open My Mouth, Open My Mind

Aerosmith, in its song "Livin' on the Edge," has these words: "There's somethin' wrong with the world today. I don't know what it is. Something's wrong with our eyes. We're seein' things in a different way. And God knows it ain't his."[4]

I know most preachers do not begin a devotion or a sermon quoting Aerosmith. Yet the words are on target. There is something wrong with the world today, and the way we are seeing things today is not the way God sees it, not the way God wants us to see it. Right! Maybe I am just not in a pie-in-the-sky frame of mind today. Maybe Polly Anna left for a day. Maybe I am just absolutely heartbroken that the world just does not get it.

What do I mean? Did you know that America has only 4.25 percent of the world's population yet we have 32 percent of the COVID-19 cases and 25 percent of the deaths worldwide? We, the country with the greatest health care and technology, are leading the world in losing the fight against this virus. We hear some politicians using the lives of our citizens as pawns to get a political advantage in the November election. We hear the politicians drowning out the scientific and medical guidance that could keep us safe. We hear too many people forming opinions based on conspiracies rather than waiting on facts. Fear is heightened! Confusion is rampant! Anger has spilled over into the streets! Where is the voice of calm? Where is the voice of reason? Where is the voice of God?

---

[4] Aerosmith, "Livin' on the Edge," songwriters Steven Tyler, Mark Hudson, and Joe Perry. Copyright by Universal Music Corp.

Look at God's Word where Solomon was preparing to dedicate the temple. God said, "When I shut up the heavens so that there is no rain, or command locusts to devour the land or send a plague among my people, if my people, who are called by my name, will humble themselves and pray and seek my face and turn from their wicked ways, then will I hear from heaven and will forgive their sin and will heal their land" (2 Chronicles 7:12–15 NIV).

Our salvation is not in the words of a president or the posturing of Congress. Our salvation is in God and God alone. It is time, and a time that is long overdue, for God's people to stand up, without picking sides in the political arena, and proclaim God's Word as God's word to guide his people back to a faith-based relationship with our Creator. There needs to be a clear call for prayer, where all people seek God's guidance. There needs to be a clear voice leading us toward humility before our God rather than arrogance. We need to be guided toward revival so we will turn away from our sins. And seek the face of God.

There's something wrong with the world today! We as Christ Followers need to point toward God who can heal our land.

In 1895, Clara Scott penned the words:

> Open my eyes, that I may see, Glimpses of truth Thou hast for Me; Place in my hands the wonderful Key That shall unclasp and set me free. Silently now I wait for Thee, Ready my God, Thy will to see, Open my eyes, illumine me, Spirit divine!

As Christ followers, God, you have asked us to be open and active in changing the wrongs in our world rather than being complainers. May we start today figuring this out in our lives. Amen.

On Top of the Mountain

In the Holy Land today, many of the most significant biblical sites are obscured from view by churches that have been built upon them. However, there are a few locations where these precious sites have not been concealed. Three that come into my mind are the Sea of Galilee, Gordon's tomb (thought to be the tomb of Jesus), and the Jezreel Valley.

At the southern end of the Jezreel Valley, while standing on top of the Har Megiddo, or the "tell" of Megiddo, with your back facing Jerusalem, you can see one of the most beautiful sights ever—145 square miles of picturesque creation. On your left is a village on the side of the mountain ridge that is Nazareth, the home of Mary, Joseph, and Jesus. Then far off in the distance, at the other end of the valley, is a mountain standing alone in the haze. This is Mount Tabor, the site of the Transfiguration of Jesus. Matthew records this experience. "After six days Jesus took with him Peter, James, and John the brother of James, and led them up a high mountain by themselves. There he was transfigured before them. His face shone like the sun, and his clothes became as white as the light. Just then there appeared before them Moses and Elijah, talking with Jesus" (Matthew 17:1–3 NIV).

Many things seem to happen on mountaintops, including Moses's encounter with God, Abraham and Isaac's experience, and the temple being built on a mountaintop. Even God is identified with the Hebrew name El Elyon (Psalm 18:13), "the Most High" (Luke 2:14), "God in the highest" (Luke 6:35), and "you will be sons of the Most High" (Luke 6:35).

We talk in our religious languages as having a mountaintop experience. When we define what we mean so nonbelievers will understand, we say it is as if we were on top of the mountain and came into the very presence of God. It is a special moment in time when we feel closer to God than at any other time. Matthew 17 can teach us a couple things about having a top-of-the-mountain experience.

First, when we have been on top of the mountain with God, we discover the need to be responsible with that experience. Jesus told his disciples, "Do not tell anyone what you have seen" (Matthew 17:9 NIV). We are to understand everything in life through God's timing. When we are excited, is it not difficult to wait to tell someone? But maybe God wants us to come to a better understanding of what that experience means to us and to others. We need to take the time to fully comprehend what has happened.

Second, it is permissible to ask God questions. The disciples questioned Jesus more about the meaning of what they had experienced. The disciples asked him, "Why then do the teachers of the law say that Elijah must come first?" (Matthew 17:10 NIV). We should ask questions like these. Why has this happened? What are you wanting me to do with this situation? Where are you wanting me to go with this experience? Is this a private experience for me only, or is it something I have experienced so others may benefit? Finish the experience you have had by asking God for clarity.

Dearest Heavenly Father, take us to your mountaintop. Allow us to at least see your passing glory. Encourage us through your reality. As we hold such an experience in our hearts, let us feel the fullness of you plan and follow through with your timing in mind. Amen.

Are You Sorry?

(There are times when only you can make your life better. What are you waiting for?)

One Saturday when I was in high school, I was driving really early in the morning to our family's lake house in Shelby County. I wanted to be alone and just do some fishing. Quiet time was what I was looking for, but it was not what I found. On the way, just a couple of miles from home, I dropped something. I do not even remember what it was. As I leaned over to grab whatever I had dropped, the car swerved, I hit a mailbox, and I ran a short way into someone's yard. The day had not even begun. The sun was not up enough to see. There were no lights on in the house. My first thought was *Nobody will know.* I drove on toward Highway 280, but before I arrived, an overwhelming feeling came over me. *I cannot let this go.* I turned around and went back home. My father heard me come back and came in to see what was up. I told him what had happened. He said something that has remained in the forefront of my thoughts ever since. "Son, go by that house, ring the doorbell, and tell the person what happened. Then you tell them you are sorry and are willing to pay to repair the damage. Whatever it costs, I will advance it to you, and then you will need to pay me back. This is your mess, and you will have to own it."

Own up to what you did, even if it was an accident. Express genuine regret. Be willing to pay the price for repairs. Be more careful in the future. A great definition in real life of the concept of repent! Jesus began his ministry with these words: "Repent, for the kingdom of heaven is near" (Matthew 4:17 NIV). Repentance is the most discussed life issue from the time of the original sin in Genesis all the way through Revelation. We long for the kingdom and often overlook repentance. In my mind, there are two words that are synonyms: *repent* and *change*. We see the term *repent* as a religious word, and we throw it around freely because we see it as a word for those other people who are not religious. But *change* is another matter. This word gets personal because "We do not like change!" However, they are both very similar. We would understand Jesus's message of repentance if we understood he came preaching, teaching, and demonstrating *change*.

Three quick ideas about repent/change and one idea to contemplate. First, *repent* means change the way you think. No one is perfect. Everyone has sinned. Yet Jesus says we all need to change the way we think. Six times he said in Matthew 5, "You have heard it said … but I say to you …" In another way of putting it, change the way you think (Matthew 5:21; 27; 31; 33; 38; 43). Second, *repent* means change the way you live. I am learning that this time of stay-at-home is good for us to learn how to change the way we live and even change the way we do church. Maybe, if we slowed down, we could enjoy family more, grow spiritually more, and appreciate what we have more. Third, *repent* means change the way you hope. I have hoped for many things in life, but I have learned over time the value of having hope "built on nothing less than Jesus's blood and righteousness."[5] Hope should be like Paul saying, "We can do all things through Christ who strengthens us" (Philippians 4:13). Not a hope that *maybe* things can be better. A hope that things *will* be better.

Finally, for your contemplation. *Repent* means changing your _____. You fill in the blank. What change will make your life happier? What change will draw you closer to God? What change will make you a better person to everyone you know?

God, give us the strength, the faith, and the persistence to change so our repentance will be genuine. Amen.

---

[5] Edward Mote's hymn "On Christ the Solid Rock," written in 1834.

The Challenge at Ephesus

Geographically and historically, Ephesus was one of the most interesting cities in the Mediterranean world. The strategic location caused it to be conquered and ruled by many rulers. This alone created challenges for life there. Each conquering ruler wanted to build larger and more grandiose temples and palaces. The Romans conquered Ephesus in 133 BC. They then built a temple to Artemis, considered one of the seven wonders of the ancient world. It was larger than the temple to Athena in Athens.

Into this pagan world, Paul, challenged by God, went and established a Christian ministry. In the shadow of this pagan temple and the worship of a multitude of false gods, the church at Ephesus grew and, one could say, even prospered. There were challenges though. In Revelation 2:1–7, John records that the church at Ephesus had "lost their first love" (verse 4). This alone tells of the wear and tear that struggle for existence had caused. The enthusiasm the church once had was waning. Then Paul, in writing to the church, reminds them of what is important. He offers a basic lesson on how to be a church.

He seems to speak of the responsibilities of leaders in a church, yet all are to work together

> to prepare God's people for works of service, so that the
> body of Christ may be built up until we all reach unity
> in the faith and in the knowledge of the Son of God and
> become mature, attaining to the whole measure of the
> fullness of Christ. Then we will no longer be infants,
> tossed back and forth by the waves, and blown here and

there by every wind of teaching and by the cunning and craftiness of men in their deceitful scheming. Instead, speaking the truth in love, we will in all things grow up into him who is the Head, that is, Christ. From him the whole body, joined and held together by every supporting ligament, grows and builds itself up in love, as each part does its work. (Ephesians 4:12–16 NIV)

Oops! Have we stumbled on something that we have not noticed before? Is this passage saying that the body of Christ has a goal and purpose, maybe even a divine plan, to be unified in our faith? How is this unity to be achieved? The leadership, no matter the role or function, no matter the seemingly importance of a position, is to prepare God's people for works of service. We are to do something!

OK, let me process through this concept another way. Consider this: If God's people are being God's people, doing God's work in God's way, in a world lost in sin, then we are not only being the church. We are *unified* as a church.

Could this then give us a whisper of an idea that this might be what Jesus was saying through John in Revelation 2 to the church at Ephesus? Is this the elusive "forsaken your first love" (Revelation 2:4 NIV)? Could they have become so consumed with the pressures of the day that they retreated into themselves rather than seeing the world around them as God's field "ripe for harvest" (John 4:35 NIV)? I think so. What say you? May we always be God's people doing God's work God's way in a world lost in sin.

> Dear God who loves us more than we deserve, assist us in our journey of faith so we might become more mature in our Christian way of interpreting what is going on in our world. May we faithfully represent your love, forgiveness, peace, and grace as we unify as believers to reach this world with the truth of Jesus. Amen.

The Effect of Friends and Places

The friends we keep and the places we go affect our lives, our attitudes, our actions, and yes, even our faith in Jesus. There is a real dichotomy in trying to live faithfully as Christ followers. On the one hand, unbelievers can truly affect our lives in many ways. They can pressure us into being less faithful. They can cause us to stray away from church and even our devotion to Christ. On the other hand, we are charged with "going into all of the world" (Matthew 28:18–20) as witnesses for Christ. How can we be faithful believers with such a contrast and with what seems to be an insurmountable conflict that affects us so greatly? Let's look at some ideas.

As confident persons of faith, we should be the influence on others rather than being influenced by others. Paul says to Timothy, "He must also have a good reputation with outsiders, so that he will not fall into disgrace and into the devil's trap" (1 Timothy 3:7 NIV). Most of us find it easier to avoid people with whom we disagree. We even talk about them in disparaging ways. We need to be the examples they are looking for as a positive change in their lives. What a complement it would be for someone to say, "I saw God's love and acceptance in your life." Worthy goal.

As proud persons of faith, we have good friends who encourage and help us stay focused. The beloved disciple said, "If we claim to have fellowship with him yet walk in the darkness, we lie and do not live by the truth. But if we walk in the light, as he is in the light, we have fellowship with one another, and the blood of Jesus, his Son, purifies us from all sin" (1 John 1:6–7 NIV). When we are in the world yet trying not to be of the world, we need support, encouragement, and friends who will encourage and strengthen us. Do you think Christ established the church just to make us feel good on Sunday? No! The church is to be the place we find the recharging of our souls for the week ahead. It is our respite for the week past. We need each other!

As determined persons of faith, we stand daily in the light of Jesus. When we are witnessing or trying to have a positive influence on a person who might not be a believer, we must stay out of the darkness. Jesus said, "While I am in the world, I am the light of the world" (John 9:5 NIV). Is this what Christ wants me to do? Is this where Christ wants me to be? Am I reflecting the light of Christ? Constant reminders of who we are and whose we are. Living in the light *always!*

As mature persons of faith, we live life with anticipation.

> Brothers, I do not consider myself yet to have taken hold of it. But one thing I do: Forgetting what is behind and straining toward what is ahead, I press on toward the goal to win the prize for which God has called me heavenward in Christ Jesus. All of us who are mature should take such a view of things. And if on some point you think differently that too God will make clear to you. (Philippians 3:13–15 NIV)

Do not give up! Do not quit! Do not quit because of your failures! Learn from where you have been and be that positive influence on others.

The friends you keep and the places you go affect your life, your attitude, your actions, and yes, even your faith in Jesus. On the other hand, the friends you keep and the places you go should affect others' lives, others' attitudes, others' actions, and yes, others' faith in the Jesus you love and trust.

God of peace and joy, make me a channel of blessing to others today. Amen.

When in Fear, the Response Is Flight or Fight Right? Run or Take a Stand? Well, Not Always

I remember times when I took risks with no fear in my mind. At the time, the experience far outweighed any thought of fear. One of these risks was holding on to a death tree and leaning out over a five-hundred-foot cliff in the Rocky Mountains to get a photograph. It was the only way to take that picture. Today, when I look at that picture, I do not see the beauty I saw then. I only see, in my mind's eye, what could have happened. Maturity, or perhaps age, causes me to see life differently. Although I might—no, never mind. I would not!

Look at these three scriptures that tell how God chooses for us to face fear: Exodus 14:15, Luke 17:14, and Acts 1:11. "Then the Lord said to Moses, 'Why are you crying out to me? Tell the Israelites to move on'" (Exodus 14:15 NIV). This often overlooked passage has always piqued my curiosity. Let's follow it through. The Egyptian army is coming in hot pursuit. God provides a fire to slow them down. The people's backs are against the Red Sea. There is nowhere to go. They are trapped. Then here it is. When all seems impossible, God says to move on. The impression to me is that only after the people began to move did Moses hold up his staff and only then did the sea part. Get it? The people needed to prove to God that they were willing to move on first, even when things seemed impossible. Get over your fear, move forward, and God can do great things!

"When he saw them, he said, 'Go, show yourselves to the priests.' And as they went, they were cleansed" (Luke 17:14 NIV). Ten men with leprosy asked to be healed. Then follow me with this. Jesus said, "Go," as if they were already healed. In his mind, they were. But here is the place we need to see clearly: "as they went, they were healed." Jesus seems to be demonstrating again that when we begin to do what God wants us to do, miracles happen on the way. Move on; go; be doing; go forward. Get it? You cannot just stand there and wait for God to give you what you desire. You need to demonstrate your faith. In the midst of the impossible, before healing comes, move!

There is the beauty hidden in these words. "'Men of Galilee,' they said, 'why do you stand here looking into the sky? This same Jesus, who has been taken from you into heaven, will come back in the same way you have seen him go into heaven'" (Acts 1:11 NIV). Those who were the most trusted followers, the ones Jesus had challenged to go into all the world, those who knew all the insights of truth in scripture, those who would tell the story for all of us to read, stood frozen longing for Christ to reappear. Or at least they were frozen in grief.

I want to challenge the church today, not just Lakeview Baptist but all churches, to see the challenge that comes out weaving these three passages together. We are facing the impossible. We are facing the pure need for a miracle. We are facing a time when we wish Christ would return. It seems to me the lesson the Bible teaches us is to *move on, get going, and stop gazing into the clouds!* We need to figure out how to move forward. As we move forward, we will encounter God's will for his church. It will not, nor should it, be the same as it once was. Israelites discovered new land (the Promised Land). Those with disease discovered healing. Those who stopped gazing experienced the Holy Spirit.

God of great challenges, give us the motivation to get up and get going so the church will be on the move! Amen.

Why Do We Do That?

Miss Winnie Yates was a dear friend in our church in Leitchfield, Kentucky. She was in her eighties and well weathered by time. She, however, never lost her joy, which overflowed from her faith in Jesus. Her two-room home looked like a home painted by Norman Rockwell of a typical poor farmhouse just following the Great Depression. A barn and a garden were in the back. Most of what she ate she grew in that garden. She was a proud woman who never traveled more than thirty miles from her home, yet she was a powerful spokesperson for supporting world missions. Her title was WMU director. This just did not capture the full extent of what she meant to Liberty Baptist Church. Many of those Kentucky rural folks would have an allotted portion of ground to grow tobacco. When the tobacco went to market, they paid their tithes and offerings with the funds received. Not Miss Winnie. When her garden came in, she canned vegetables for the year. If she canned ten quarts of tomatoes, beans, okra, or whatever, one jar went to the pastor and his family. "I do not have much, but I give 10 percent to the pastor as my gift back to God for all God has given to me," she once told me.

There are many aspects of spirituality. All are vital for Christians to stay connected with our faith and to follow faithfully our Lord's desires. We see many of these elements in a worship service. Things like prayer, praise, Bible reading, fellowship, and the opportunity to make choices in our journey. One we often do not emphasize more highly is giving our tithes and offerings. You hear us say we need to pay for such and such or you hear us say we have this special offering, but you do not hear us say enough, "Have you been faithful this week with your stewardship?"

God says, "Will a man rob God? Yet you rob me. But you ask, "How do we rob you?" In tithes and offerings" (Malachi 3:8 NIV). He then goes on to say he will open the floodgates from heaven and bless us. Then the challenge of "Test me in this" (Malachi 3:10 NIV). There are also the stories of Jesus regarding stewardship, such as in 1 Corinthians 4:1–2, Matthew 23:23, and Luke 11:42. All seem to be indicators that stewardship is more than just giving dollars. It is being faithful with what God has entrusted us with so we are more effectively able to serve him and his concept of "seeking and saving that which is lost" (Luke 19:10 NIV).

Just something to think, pray, and consider committing yourself to so you can expand your expression of faith. What does a faithful commitment to stewardship (at least tithing) accomplish for the follower of Christ? It allows you to prioritize your life by saying, "This is the thing of first importance in my life." It is like seeking first the kingdom of God. It allows you to feel you are a part of more than who you are individually, and it plugs you into the work of God's kingdom. It presents the opportunity for you to eternally feel that although you were not able to do much, you were a faithful steward. Whether the church's ministry needs it or there is a goal set for something special, you need to have a clear understanding that you need to sacrificially give more. The church needs it, you need to be a participant in church dreams, and the goal needs to be surpassed. Be a faithful steward. Test God in this and see his blessings.

Was Miss Winnie rich? Not in earthly terms. But she was one of the richest persons I have ever known. Rich in her devotion and faithfulness to serving God. How do you want to be remembered?

Giver of all things, even life itself, help me to appreciate what you have provided for me. Giver of all things, help me to learn to demonstrate through my faithfulness and stewardship just how much I appreciate all you are and all you have done. Amen.

Sometimes the Bible Causes Me to Struggle

We live in an ever-increasing society of hate. I began to mature and see what was going on in the world with my own eyes during the 1960s. There were conflicts on college campuses over the Vietnam War; there were riots in Birmingham over desegregation, church bombings, and crosses being burned. Yet I believe the fires of hate and the anger over disagreements of all kinds are burning just as brightly today, if not more so. This obvious hatred causes me, as a Christian and as a human being, to struggle emotionally and even physically. It is one thing that keeps me up at night. So maybe I should stop here and wait to write this. No, I feel the compulsion to get it out of my system and put it in print for all of us who struggle with in our souls.

There was a point, and everyone needs to determine when that point was for themselves, that dialogue in America became more of "I have got to win" rather than "I want to hear all sides." Then the ultimate choice was made when we began believing that if someone disagrees with me, or my favorite personality, then I hate them. They must be wrong. Thus, we now have a system in America where we are so polarized in all aspects of our society that we have created an abyss so wide and so deep there will be no survivors if we try to find middle ground. This happens in churches, politics, debates around coffee tables, and even families. Friendships are broken. It's as if we are fighting a new civil war, this time with words and anger. Hatred causes more isolation than COVID-19.

So allow me to toss a biblical issue into this as a way to demonstrate what I am talking about. Ready? "The crusades were fought to 'free the holy Land' from the evil Islamic Empire." That is a quote from Thomas S. Asbridge's *The First Crusade: A New History* (a very good book). This created a great divide between the Muslims and Christians. Catapult your thoughts to the tragic event that occurred on September 11, 2001. This was the day when we experienced an attack in America by a few radical Islamic terrorists in four planes. Suddenly, we entered a season of distrust and hatred of all Muslims. But what about Jesus's challenge to "love your enemies and pray for those who persecute you" (Matthew 5:44 NIV)? We would rather go to psalms where the psalmist says, "In your unfailing love, silence my enemies; destroy all my foes" (Psalm 143:12 NIV). Then to complicate things even more, look back at Genesis, where God says to Abraham, because Abraham was worried about the future of Ishmael, "I will make the son of the maidservant into a nation also, because he is your offspring" (Genesis 21:13 NIV). Then in Genesis 21:17, God sent an angel to save Hagar and Ishmael in the desert and repeated the promise of making him into a great nation. We do not often put all of this into one thought pattern.

So here is what I want us to consider in our prayers: What does God want us to do when we disagree? Maybe it is to see the whole story in its completeness and find room for discussions rather than distance. With Holy Scripture, we must struggle with what it means that God blessed Ishmael. I am not sure I understand all that's in that part, but struggle is necessary. We must see the reference in Psalm 143 as David's cry. We must see Jesus's words in Matthew 5:44 as a command from God. See, life is not so easy. Being a Christ follower was never meant to be an easy road. Jesus did say to "take up your cross" (Mark 10:21 NKJV), right? How are we to deal with issues? Struggle to find God's truth, not justifications for our prejudices.

On any issue, in any environment, with any group of people, no one has the perfect answer. If we cannot share our personal opinions without the fear of being ostracized, we can never find God's will; we will only have one person's opinion. Get it? Or am I just verbalizing my personal frustrations?

God of grace and God of glory, bring peace into the world. Use us as instruments of your love. There are many things and truths in your Word that cause us to struggle. Help us to find your truth free from our prejudices. Amen.

Buckle Up Your Chin Strap!

There is a time in the sport of football when you are facing a difficult foe and someone will say, "It's time to buckle up your chin straps and get ready to play the game of your life!" I heard these words from many coaches through the years. Spiritually, emotionally, mentally, and as a church, that time is here. We are so easily distracted from who we are and what we are supposed to be doing in the world we live in. God's message is vitally important for our time now. I have always enjoyed the phrase "We need to be doing God's work, God's way, in God's time, in a world that is lost in sin." This time away from God's house of prayer has been a perfect opportunity to regain our focus. It is time to connect in new ways with our community. It is time to reenvision God's plan for the church. It is time to buckle up our chin straps and get ready to play the game of our lives.

The simple, short, often overlooked book of Jude hits me between the eyes like a sledgehammer. If we can absorb its truth, this little book can revolutionize our faith and the church's purpose. "Dear friends, although I was very eager to write to you about the salvation we share, I felt I had to write and urge you to contend for the faith that was once for all entrusted to the saints" (Jude 1:3 NIV). Then toward the end we find

> But you, dear friends, build yourselves up in your most holy faith and pray in the Holy Spirit. Keep yourselves in God's love as you wait for the mercy of our Lord Jesus Christ to bring you to eternal life. Be merciful to those who doubt; snatch others from the fire and save them; to others show mercy, mixed with fear—hating even the clothing stained by corrupted flesh. (Jude 1:20–23 NIV)

"Contend for the faith" (Jude 1:3 NIV). *Struggle, resist, deal with, compete, challenge, run, put yourself forward*: words in a thesaurus to explain the word *contend*. Pick your word or words. They all seem to say we need to be active. In a progressive way making sure we are in the game, not watching from a distance. Tropical storms and hurricanes come onto the shores of our country and leave behind destruction, death, and chaos. They also erode the shoreline; the beaches are washed away. If we did not have plans to rebuild the beaches, there would be less and less beach. Property values would change, and our joy of being beach bums would be lost.

When crisis comes from external and internal forces in a church, these crises cause our foundation of faith to begin to crumble and erode. We slip into a survival mode rather than an attitude of boldly proclaiming our faith. God *never* intended for his church to just survive. It is not our business to just "keep the doors open." We, as God's church, are to thrive. This is where we buckle up and rediscover ways to thrive no matter what. Contend for the faith, as Jude said!

Look at some words used in verses 20–23 again. "Build yourselves up! Pray in the holy Spirit! Live in God's love! Wait or anticipate eternal life! Be merciful! Save sinners! Show mercy!" (Jude 1:20–23 NIV). You tell me. Do these words indicate just sitting on the pew? Do these words call us to just survive? Do these words plead for us to be passive? I say no. Somehow, we must buckle up get in the game of our lives so our community connects with the idea that we are a lighthouse of hope. Pray with me about this! Struggle with the idea of what we are to look like as we go forth in the days ahead. We cannot, should not, and will not be the same! But we must always be God's church guided by God's plan!

God, it was your plan for our church to come into existence. You had a plan then that was fitting for the time. We know you have a plan now that is fitting for the twenty-first century. Help us to discover what you intend for us today so we can actively follow your guidance and not our own. Amen.

Light versus Dark: Is It That Big of a Deal?

Do you think Ichabod Crane would have been so fear-struck by Washington Irving's headless horseman in "The Legend of Sleepy Hollow" if their encounter had been in the daytime and he could have seen, in the light of day, that the pumpkin was not a real head? Yes, this light versus dark is a big deal!

Nighttime, thus the dark, has always been depicted in history as evil, mainly because people can be unseen in the dark and evil deeds can take place without others knowing the culprit. This concept of darkness and evil has carried over in the spiritual world to help illustrate the contrast between goodness and evil, thus God and Satan. Before God created the world, "the earth was formless and empty, darkness was over the surface" (Genesis 1:2 NIV). "And God said, 'Let there be light'" (Genesis 1:3 NIV). Light brings life and beauty and pushes the darkness away. John said, "In him was life, and that life was the light of men" (John 1:4 NIV). Jesus said, "I am the light of the world. Whoever follows me will never walk in darkness but will have the light of life" (John 8:12 NIV)

We could go on with this thought, but I want us to focus on John 3:10–21. Jesus said, "Everyone who does evil hates the light, and will not come into the light for fear that his deeds will be exposed. But whoever lives by the truth comes into the light, so that it may be seen plainly that what he has done has been done through God" (John 3:20–21 NIV)

Jesus had just told Nicodemus about God so loving the world that he gave his Son, and this is where we find our salvation, the redemption for the death sentence due to our sins (John 3:16–17 NIV). Now Jesus is declaring what happens after a person makes a decision, a commitment, a choice to follow him. Change takes place. A change that is obvious to others. Faith becomes actionable. When we walk into the light, we do so so that our deeds will be seen as being done through our newfound faith in God (John 3:17–21 NIV).

Did you see the movie *Saving Private Ryan*? It is a difficult movie to watch; as the critics said, it makes war more real than any movie up to that time. However, it is worth watching the movie. When you arrive on the bridge at the end of the movie, Private Ryan is safe. However, many men died to save him. The main character, Captain Miller, played by Tom Hanks, who is dying of a gunshot to the chest, pulls Ryan over and whispers, "James, earn this. Earn this!" Then Miller dies. The movie fades from that scene to a modern-day Private Ryan standing at the cemetery in Normandy. He turns to his wife and says, "Have I lived a good life?"

With the sacrifice Jesus made for us, the grace God gives to us, the question comes back to confront us every day. Are we earning it? Are we living a good life? That is determined by the amount of time we spend living in the light of Jesus and avoiding the dark places in this world. To receive the "Well done, good and faithful servant" (Matthew 25:23 NIV, the faithful servant parable) we must be children of light, showing through our deeds what has happened within our souls.

God of light and life, I have but a little light as compared to the light of your Son, Jesus, Assist me in being able to demonstrate each day my choice to fulfill the old song "This little light of mine, I'm going to let it shine, this little light of mine, I'm going to let it shine, let it shine, let it shine, let it shine."[6] I do this because I want to be able to say, "I lived a good life!" Amen.

---

[6] "This Little Light of Mine" written by Harry Dixon Loes in 1920.

Why Is Love So Important to God? Get Your Bibles Out for Today!

(The word sincere equals genuine, honest, truthful, earnest, heartfelt, open, serious, and authentic.)

Follow me please: A personal encounter with a loving God leads to a commitment to change your life. This commitment to change your life leads you to follow a path toward holiness. This path toward holiness leads you toward specific areas of your heart/soul. One such area, and most likely the most vital of these specific areas, is *love.* We visualize this in words like these: "Dear friends, let us love one another, for love comes from God. Everyone who loves has been born of God and knows God" (1 John 4:7 NIV).

There are so many great scriptures regarding this concept of love. Let me reference a few for you to read. John 15:9–27 assists us in understanding that love is a foundational issue of faith. First Corinthians 13:1–13 teaches a marvelous definition of Christian love that leaves no wiggle room. First John 4 identifies love as the true marker between real faith and false faith. Please take the time to read these references before proceeding.

I want to turn our attention to Romans 12. Paul, in communicating what was important for the Romans to understand, talks about this love given by God and expected from believers. He says, "Love must be sincere" (Romans 12:9 NIV). The contrast Paul uses is between good and evil. In my thoughts, it is a matter of love conquers evil while evil suppresses that which is good. The choice is left up to each of us. It is a matter of where we want to take our stand. Will we choose love, or will we fall prey to evil?

He then pivots to talk about how love affects our attitude in Romans 12:12–15. Attitude is everything, is it not? It determines how we face challenges, pain, competition, and change. One could say faith affects our attitude, and attitude is the evidence of our faith. Yes, I am meddling here. But it is true? Correct? What attitude does Paul talk about? He mentions hope, affliction, prayer, benevolence/hospitality, persecution, joy, and grief. Study how Paul uses these words.

Finally, Paul shifts in Romans 12:16–21 to say more than we can ever fully accomplish. He seems to be saying it is our responsibility to make every good effort to do it anyway. Just see these words: "If it is possible, as far as it depends on you, live at peace with everyone" (Romans 12:18 NIV). Let me be honest and forthright here. We all would rather, and most commonly do, choose to use the first part as our jumping off point. "If it is possible." We simply want to say, "Well, with that person or this person, it is not possible." But look at the middle part of verse 18. "As far as it depends on you." In my limited way of trying to figure this out, I have found myself looking in a mirror and saying, "It may be impossible for me because of … but with God's help, I had better choose to start trying."

Readers, if you do not hear anything else, hear this: love is a choice that leads to living peaceably with all people, even when it is difficult. I remember on *many* occasions when I tried to excuse my way out of being in trouble, my father would sit me down and say, "Son, there are always reasons you can give for making dumb decisions that get you in trouble, but there are no excuses."

Followers of Christ, there is a multitude of reasons we can offer for not following God's guidance, but there are no excuses. Our advocate Jesus simply says, "Did you follow my command, to love one another as I have loved you?" (John 13:34 NIV). No excuses.

God of love and peace, create in me a clean heart so I can love as you desire me to love. No excuses! Amen.

Rocking Chair Theology

Worry is like a rocking chair. It is something to do, but it will not get you anywhere. We live in a world of worriers. We can worry about anything, especially when we are not able to get out and about and stay busy. Sometimes I think we try to stay so busy just to keep the stress of worry off our minds. Then in the quietness of the night, we struggle to sleep because the worry keeps coming back. Worry is like a beach ball. We try to hold it under water just to realize we cannot keep it down forever. Jesus offers wonderful ideas and challenges in the Sermon on the Mount. One such idea is dealing with worry. In Matthew 6:24–32, he directs us to some attitudinal lifestyle changes that will enhance our living. Look at two verses in particular. "Therefore I tell you, do not worry about your life, what you will eat or drink; or about your body, what you will wear. Is not life more important than food, and the body more important than clothes?" (Matthew 6:25 NIV). "Therefore do not worry about tomorrow, for tomorrow will worry about itself. Each day has enough trouble of its own" (Matthew 6:34 NIV).

We worry about the little things so much that we do not leave enough energy to deal with the big events in life. Did you know anxiety, the result of worry, causes health issues like high blood pressure, heart disease, allergies, ulcers, etc.? Life would be more fulfilling if we spent less time on minor issues.

We worry about things we cannot control. Jesus said we worry about what we shall wear and then points to the lilies of the field. If God can produce such beauty as this, a little flower, why don't we allow him to take care of us also? Jesus jumps into our psyche and makes worry a trust issue. It is a trust issue (Matthew 6:19–25 NIV)! In my way of thinking, I can hear his soft, loving voice saying each day, when we worry, "Let God take care of this" (Matthew 6:30–34).

We worry about tomorrow so much that we miss the beauty of the moment in which we are living. There are two days you cannot do anything about: yesterday and tomorrow. Jesus said, "Do not worry about tomorrow until tomorrow gets here" (Matthew 6:34). Focus on where you are now. Is not this the very reason the Israelites were given only enough manna in the wilderness for the day? God was trying to tell them to trust him each day. Do not get ahead of yourselves. Do not cross bridges until you get to that bridge. Is not this why we have been instructed to not go out and build bigger barns (Luke 12:18)? Take the day as it comes and see what God has in store. No one is promised more than the moment of time we are living in.

We forget to put God into the picture of our lives. Jesus wants us to trust God in all matters of life. Worry is a failure to communicate with and trust God. Paul says, "And we know that in all things God works for the good of those who love him, who have been called according to his purpose" (Romans 8:28 NIV).

Holy Father of heaven and of our hearts, assist us in developing a stronger trust in you. You who created us, you who continues to love us, you who continues to guide us, you who gave your only Son to save us, you who will care for us eternally. May we trust you enough today to lessen our worry and strengthen our faith in you. Amen.

Torture! Why Did I Do It?

Every summer we would get these letters from the coach, high school and college, reminding us of the importance of getting mentally, physically, and emotionally ready for August two-a-day practices. I hated with an immense passion those terribly hot, humid, painful days. There is just no other way to put it. Well, I probably did use other terms prior to becoming a pastor. The running, the hitting, the sweat, the smells, the exhaustion—it was torture. Practice from 8:00 until 11:00, break for lunch and a little rest when you could. The sore muscles kept us from real relaxation. Then again, at 3:00 back out on the field for another three hours. Every year I would think, *Why in the world do I allow myself to go through this?* I just wanted to play the games. I looked forward to the crowds, the challenge, the excitement of winning, and hearing everyone at school talking about what happened in the games. Why can we not just play the games? Then the first game would arrive, and it seemed like every first game was a close one until the fourth quarter when it really counted. Both in high school and college, we had coaches who really worked us hard in August, and when that fourth quarter arrived, we were in better condition than most any team we played. Victory was won not so much because of what we did in the game itself but because of what we did in August. All the repetition, the conditioning, the pain, the heat, and the exhaustion paid off by getting us ready for the challenges that faced us in the season.

Jesus worked with his disciples teaching, training, and equipping them for the tasks that lay before them after his ascension. Paul said, "Do your best to present yourself to God as one approved, a workman who does not need to be ashamed and who correctly handles the word of truth" (2

Timothy 2:15 NIV). Paul also says to the church in Corinth, "I gave you milk, not solid food, for you were not yet ready for it. Indeed, you are still not ready" (1 Corinthians 3:2 NIV). There is this constant emphasis on studying, growing, maturing, and developing as Christ followers. Why? Christianity has constantly been a faith in crisis. Christ himself was constantly confronted by folks who "stirred up the people" (Acts 6:12 NIV). There was and is persecution. There have always been false prophets. There have been times of sluggishness of faith.

If we are not equipped and ready to handle stress, challenges, disappointments, and confusion as faith believers, we will lose the challenges we face in life. This is why we should constantly be maturing and equipping ourselves for the big challenges we will most certainly all face. Remember Paul saying, "Not only so, but we also rejoice in our sufferings, because we know that suffering produces perseverance; perseverance, character; and character, hope. And hope does not disappoint us, because God has poured out his love into our hearts by the Holy Spirit, whom he has given us (Romans 5:3–5 NIV).

How do we do this? Jesus said, "You diligently study the Scriptures because you think that by them you possess eternal life. These are the Scriptures that testify about me" (John 5:39 NIV). Study God's Word. Be a prayer warrior like Jesus. Fellowship with other Christ followers. Learn how to share your faith. Determine your God-given gifts and use them. When a new crisis comes, you will then be prepared for the joy of being overcomers, or as one might say, enjoying the victory due to the hard work that you put into the preparation. This is why the church is vital. It helps us get ready for a life of faith.

It is game time, people! How prepared are you?

Father of discipline and love, guide us through the perils of life, and to hold on to your truths, which will always bring us victory over the challenges we face. Help us to be prepared for life, and keep our focus on you. Amen.

I Need a Break! Have You Checked Your Pulse Today?

Last week your church staff recorded the Mother's Day service on Tuesday evening, our regular day to record. We were recording due to the shutdown caused by COVID-19. I must confess I did not feel well that day. I felt weak and run-down. Becky had said that morning we needed to get away for a couple of days. Take a break and go to the beach or to the mountains. On Wednesday morning, I wrote my daily devotion and posted it. I went downstairs for breakfast and walked the dog. I felt so weak that I told Becky I needed to lie down. Suddenly, I began to feel as if I was about to pass out. I had Becky check my blood pressure and pulse. It was a strange feeling to not get a blood pressure on the first try, then to find out my heart rate was forty. We called my cardiologist, and he sent us to the emergency room at a Birmingham hospital. Why go to the mountains or the beach when the hospital is closer?

After tests and monitoring, it was determined my heart rate was in the low thirties at night, and I was in need of a pacemaker. So here I am back at the computer today writing this devotion with a perfect heart rate. As anyone who has a pacemaker can tell you, I do not feel any activity that is abnormal, but it is a curious thing to think about mini bolts of lightning going through small wires to my heart while stimulating the most essential organ in my body, causing it to function properly. I am grateful for being back to normal but a little awestruck. Crisis comes to us all.

This sidetrack in my life's journey has helped me appreciate the dedicated doctors, nurses, and all the hospital staff in what they are doing during this COVID-19 crisis. They are helping the patients with emergencies as they arise, as well as the virus patients. They are helping people in a medical crisis to be safe yet treated as needed. How blessed we are to have people in the front lines who are putting themselves at risk to follow their calling. I was amazed and impressed.

In Acts 16 we have the story of Paul and his companions traveling, doing God's work until they arrived at Troas. They were here in Troas due to being prevented by the Spirit of Christ. "Paul and his companions traveled throughout the region of Phrygia and Galatia, having been kept by the Holy Spirit from preaching the word in the province of Asia. When they came to the border of Mysia, they tried to enter Bithynia, but the Spirit of Jesus would not allow them to. So they passed by Mysia and went down to Troas" (Acts 16:5–8 NIV). Wait a minute! That's not how we were taught to deal with events that sidetrack us from what we plan to do. Blame it on Jesus! No, that does not sound correct! That's when we have to, as Paul Harvey so famously said, "See the rest of the story." Further in Acts 16:9–10, Paul tells how while he was stopped in his tracks, he received a vision of a man in Macedonia saying, "Come and help us" (Acts 16:9 NIV). So due to this crisis in Paul's life the Gospel was brought into Europe and continued to spread. It is part of the theme of Acts, "the unhindered Gospel" (Acts 28:31).

How do you look at events that sidetrack you from what you want to do? I sense we are looking inside Paul's heart. In retrospect he dictates to Luke this story. He realized as life unfolded it had to have been the Spirit of Jesus that hindered them so he would be ready for the plans that Jesus had in store for them. Is this the way we should think about life? I think yes.

I wish I had received a different inheritance from my parents than heart-related issues. Yet that is what they left for me. I wish I had not had to deal with low heart rate, yet this is what happened. I wish it had not happened during this time in my life and in the life of the church, yet that is what happened. So I have learned from Paul to recognize that Jesus may be hindering me from doing what I wanted to do, for what he is planning for us. I cannot wait to see what will be next as we as a family of faith begin to figure out how to meet together safely. We will be putting together the pieces of the church of the future. What a vision!

> God who leads us through life with a purpose, give us a vision of what's next for your followers and for your church. When this crisis is over, what plans do you have? Amen.

Nine Stones That Cause Us to Stumble: Are You a Happy Person Today? Be Honest!

I t truly was one of the most beautiful days we experienced on our trip to the Holy Land. The bus we were traveling in stopped on top of a hill with a breathtaking view of the Sea of Galilee. Our tour guide, Jim McCain, was telling us, "Look, over there across the Sea; that was where the swine were driven into the sea by Jesus. To your left was Capernaum, the place mentioned so often where Jesus spent time ministering." We walked by a large building on top of the hill, surrounded by magnificent gardens. This he described as a hostel, a place where people who are on a religious journey stay for rest and inspiration. Then we walked around to the side of the hill. I was thinking it was to just take in the beauty of the place. We sat down, and here is what we were told: "Each of you look closely at the tiny wildflowers that are growing at this time of year. These wildflowers are called lilies of the field." Then our tour guide quoted from scripture. "And why do you worry about clothes? See how the lilies of the field grow. They do not labor or spin" (Matthew 6:28 NIV). Peaceful, beautiful, historic, and suddenly, we realized we were sitting on the very mountainside where Jesus taught the Sermon on the Mount (Matthew 5–7; Luke 6). We read together the first portion called the beatitudes. Nine times Jesus says "blessed" or "blest." The Greek word is *makarios*. The better translation is happy. How many times when we are out in the community has someone said, "Have a blessed day"? I want to respond by saying, "If you are blessed, you need to be a blessing." I have begun saying, "Do you know the Greek definition of *blessed?*" It usually causes a discussion regarding if we are really happy.

Look at these nine "happy statements" with me. First, look at the nine groups of people that Jesus mentions: poor in spirit (weak faith), grief stricken (mourning), meek (humble), seekers of righteousness (want to do the right thing), merciful (caregivers), pure in heart (life is open book), peacemakers (stop anger and hatred), persecuted (despised for what they believe), and run down by others (disliked or hated for whatever reason) (Matthew 5:3–10 NIV). Do you see the similarity? Well, I am going to tell you my idea here. Everyone, whether by life's circumstances of crisis or criticized for your personal beliefs, can feel lonely and lost, which brings on sadness and despair.

Yet in every situation that seems overwhelming to all of us at some point, God brings us reasons to be happy. Just, for an example, look at verses 3–4 and allow me to paraphrase. Those who are still weak in their faith can be happy because God's kingdom is still available for them. Those who are grief stricken can find happiness because it is only through God's grace found in Jesus that we will find true comfort. The issue is finding happiness as a follower of Christ in all situations. Are you a happy person today? Be honest!

What are those nine reasons for the nine groups of people? Gift of God's kingdom; comfort; inheritance; filled with what we are seeking; receive back all the mercy we give away; see God; being God's children, again, receiving the kingdom of heaven; great is our reward in heaven. Get it! Notice how so many challenges in life are focused on the temporary and how many things that bring happiness are focused on the eternal. Do you think that maybe Jesus is foreshadowing his teaching? "But seek first his kingdom and his righteousness, and all these things will be given to you as well" (Matthew 6:33 NIV).

Put life into proper perspective. Do not try to serve two masters (Matthew 6:24). Interpret life by the eternal blessings that bring you happiness rather than the things of this world or other people's attitudes in this world. God is in control; he loves us through life and holds the door open for his kingdom.

God of happiness, joy, peace, and hope, broaden our mental and spiritual concepts to find happiness in this world because of the confidence in the world that is to come. Amen.

Going Too Far

Is there a time in your life that you simply wish would disappear from your memory? The time I experienced that was one of the worst of my memories. (There were others I choose not to share). The memory I refer to today is an experience during my freshman year of college. I had turned down a couple of scholarships to major colleges to sign with Samford University, due to a promise I had made to my sister. Then that summer, prior to school starting, I had an accident that caused a recurrence of an injury. I gave up the scholarship and, in a sense, gave up on myself. I was not a good student that fall. Additionally, I was doing things that I knew were wrong, which created a massive tension between my parents and me. There was a big confrontation where my father laid down the law. "Either you do what I say and receive money from me or you are on your own!" I will not go into the unfortunate things I said. Just in summary, I walked out declaring my independence and accepting total separation from family. As I left, my father said, "Anytime you want to come home, the door will be opened, and a light will be on to show you the way to our love." My thought then was *I wish he had just yelled*. Over the next six months, I proved to myself I could make it on my own. I got a job. I worked at schoolwork. And against medical advice, I went out for football in the spring to pay my way through school. I would, however, every now and then drive by my house late at night to see if that light was really on. It was. Never out. Always a beacon of hope and offer of restoration.

One day my father was in the hospital. I realized I needed to go see him and try to piece things together. I walked into his room and said something, trying to say what needed to be said, when he stopped me and said, "Son, I am proud of how you have proven you can make it on your own. Let's just move on from here." Nothing was ever said again about that awful time in our lives. Nothing! However, there is *always* a light that shines in our house reminding me of that moment in time and telling my family that they are always welcome to come home.

That was my life experience where I learned by a parable in real life what sin was, what sin causes, what sin brings with it, and how our Father in heaven forgives all sin. That is, when we are willing to come home. Paul says this: "For the wages of sin is death, but the gift of God is eternal life in Christ Jesus our Lord" (Romans 6:23 NIV). "What shall we say, then? Shall we go on sinning so that grace may increase? By no means! We died to sin; how can we live in it any longer?" (Romans 6:1–2 NIV). Also read Romans 3:21–26, where we find these words: "We are all sinners."

Sin is predictable. We are all sinners. Left to our own devises, and in our own self-defiance, we will do stupid things. We lose our focus on what is right. We lose our focus on God. Sin causes heartbreak. It causes heartbreak in families and from the family of faith (our church). The heartbreak of sin leaves us on the outside praying to see that light burning even when we are still on the outside. Sin causes separation. Separation from those we love and those who love us. The loneliness of separation created by sin brings issues of its on. We spiral down to cover the hurt of the pain of loneliness.

"But the gift of God is eternal life through Jesus Christ our Lord" (Romans 6:23). My father, the prodigal's father, and our Heavenly Father are always waiting to accept us back. The light to welcome us home is always lit. All we have to do is walk into the room, present ourselves humble, even if we stumble as to what to say and how to say it. In my mind's eye, I hear God saying as my father said, "Son, I am proud of how you have proven you can make it on your own. Let's just move on from here."

Father of all the universe, forgive me, accept me, welcome me, and leave the light on for me. Amen.

How High Are Your Goals?
How Focused Are Your Visions?

Paul said, "Our hope is in the Living God, who is the Savior of all, and especially to those who believe" (1 Timothy 4:9 NIV). When we want to improve professionally, physically, or even mentally, we should set our goals so high that we can only accomplish them with divine help. Then each step of the way we will see progress toward our goals, even if we do not fully accomplish them. When our "hope" is in God through Jesus Christ, we should be striving each day to reach eternal goals.

So many people today have lost a sense of direction; they have lost *hope.* This is true for Christians, and it is true for Christian churches. Where are we going? How are we going to get there? What is the purpose in what we are doing? Where is God's plan in all of this? These are questions we all should be attempting to answer and struggle with daily. If we want to be living the way God challenges us to live, we must struggle with questions such as these. It is a matter of life or death for our faith and our churches. I love the old story I heard years ago about the man in a small town who was known as the best shot in the county. All over the county were bull's-eyes painted on fence posts, old barns, walls, and any other objects where it was safe enough for there to be a target. In the absolute dead center of every target was a bullet hole. This man seemingly could not miss. A reporter came to town to interview "the perfect shooter." "How can you be so perfect? How long did it take you to reach perfection? Who was your teacher?" The old gentleman pushed back on his front porch swing, smiled, then began his answer. "Well, sir, it is this way. You shoot where you want to shoot. Then you find the bullet hole, and you paint the target over the hole, so it is perfect!" Then the old man began to laugh, but the reporter did not laugh. He simply turned and walked away.

Is this the way we live our lives? Is this the way we "do church"? Do we just shoot and whatever we hit, say that is what I was aiming for? Sure, some might say you are a perfect shot, but you are not really. Or do we live a hope-filled, targeted life with goals so high only with God's help can we accomplish them. If the second option is what you desire, then you will give God the glory for all the accomplishments you have in life rather than being so self-centered. We preachers could learn a great deal about humility if we followed this principle. I find my challenge here. Are you listening to yourself, Buddy?

Hope and determination are the engines that drive the ship of our lives. When we are focused on hope and we set out our targets prior to moving forward, we are entering the movement toward perfection. The end result may very well be the most sought-after compliment anyone could receive. "Well done, good and faithful servant! You have been faithful with a few things; I will put you in charge of many things. Come and share your master's happiness!" (Matthew 25:21 NIV).

Targeted determination and a focus-filled life all begin with the absolute hope found in Jesus Christ. It is he who drives us toward perfection! It is he who lifts us up when we stumble! It is he who fills our souls with, as a seminary professor used to say, a stubborn stick-to-itiveness, for we are all doing God's work in a world that desperately needs what Christ has to offer! It is he who drives us toward perfection! How high are your goals? How focused are your visions? Are your spiritual batteries fully charged with hope?

God of second and third chances, may the eyes of our hearts be enlightened that we may know what it is to live with the true hope found only in your Son, Jesus. Amen.

What to Say Today?

I sat at my computer today with a blank slate again. I really mean it. I have a million thoughts running through my head all day, every day, until this morning. I prepare to share some insight into life and faith and then it happens: *nothing.* I guess my brain cells have been running their own race of life and have become so exhausted that they just are on strike today. Then it happens! I am looking in my Bible, the one I have used since January 7, 2007, and come across the verses so often overlooked yet I had marked as vital: John 1:17–18. It is not overlooked because of insignificance. It is simply where it is in the Bible. John has given us the beautiful "In the beginning was the word …" (John 1:1). He talks about God and Jesus being one. He talks about light and life. He talks about John the Baptist. Then he declares, "The Word became flesh and made his dwelling among us" (John 1:2–16). All of this is what captures our attention and creates an opportunity to not read further. Read these verses twice before continuing: "For the law was given through Moses; grace and truth came through Jesus Christ. No one has ever seen God, but God the One and Only, who is at the Father's side, has made him known" (John 1:17–18 NIV).

Moses set out God's rules and regulations with the presentation of the Ten Commandments. These laws are there so we know when we step over the lines God has set to keep us on track. When we step over those lines, we call it sin. However, when Jesus came, the light of grace and truth began to shine. Grace, the free gift of God for salvation and forgiveness, was given to erase our indiscretions and keep us on track, out of humble appreciation and a determination to become better (radical change standing in the light of Christ; Acts 9:1–7). The truth Jesus brings is seen in the clear understanding of who we really are (lost in sin; Romans 3:23), whose we should be (for God so loved the world; John 3:16), and the actions we need to take to connect with the one who offers life and life beyond our expectations. Get it.

This leads us to what comes next.

Here comes the twist. This part hit me between the eyes this morning. "No one has seen God, but He has been made known" (John 1:18; John 6:46; 1 John 4:12 NIV). We will not know what God looks like until we arrive in heaven. Jesus came to allow us a glimpse of what God is like. In him all the qualities of God were walking around in human flesh. The love, the forgiveness, the humility, the peace, the calming effect, the miraculous, the fatherly image, the servant attitude, the compassion for the poor, the willingness to think more of others than self, and on the list could go.

Here is the challenge that pierced my heart when I was reading this morning. The blank slate began to burst forth with images needed to comprehend the fullness of the meaning of this statement. In Acts 11:26, we find that believers were first called Christians in Antioch. The translation of the term Christian is "little Christ." If Jesus came to give us a glimpse of what God is like, if we are to be Christlike, if we are followers of Christ, then is it not our newfound life's responsibility to show to the world a glimpse of what God is like? Go look in the mirror this morning and ask yourself, "Do I show others a glimpse of what God is like? What can I do today to show more of God to others? When I see myself, when I look deep within my soul, when I review my actions from yesterday, what do I see and feel?"

Oh beautiful, loving, compassionate Father in heaven, help me to put my ambitions, my loves, my desires, and my direction in second place and put your ambitions for me, your loves for me, your desires for me, and your directions for me in first place. May I become less of a poor reflection of you and more of a clear picture of who you really are. Let me be a proper glimpse, to those I see today, of your grace and truth. Amen.

My Story, Not Yours!

cannot speak to the calling of another person. A person's calling has to be interpreted as an event between him/her and God. I can only speak to how God moved me when I was struggling with whether to pursue ministry. In my case, as I experienced it with my limited understanding, it was a calling, not a job or career choice. However, in whatever way God chooses to reach down and touch our lives individually, it affects the way we interpret life from that point forward.

During the time Becky and I were engaged, I began struggling with how I was going to balance my life with career, faith, family, and all the things I wanted to do and accomplish. Since I was a believer in God's grace, though not very devoted to his principles, I began for the first time to study scripture. The small column with the brass plaque in front of the Samford University library had this verse: "Study to shew thyself approved unto God, a workman that needeth not to be ashamed, rightly dividing the word of truth" (2 Timothy 2:15 KJV). I saw it almost every day walking through campus. It had been burned into my psyche. So I began to study God's Word.

One day, two passages stuck in my thoughts. First was this: "He replied, 'You of little faith, why are you so afraid?' Then he got up and rebuked the winds and the waves, and it was completely calm" (Matthew 8:26 NIV). Then was this: "He replied, 'Because you have so little faith. I tell you the truth, if you have faith as small as a mustard seed, you can say to this mountain, "Move from here to there" and it will move. Nothing will be impossible for you'" (Matthew 17:20 NIV). Somehow, in some miraculous way, I felt as if God was implying I knew I was meant to be a minister. The problem is not the winds and waves in your life; it is a faith issue. I began to understand I simply needed to take the first step of faith, just a little faith, and God will lead me the rest of the way. To experience a moment of calling, I knew I needed to surrender, trust God, and have the confidence that the faith I had was enough to start this journey of ministry. Some people said because my father was a pastor it was easy for me to become a minister. Not. Some have said I was following in my father's footsteps. Not. Being my father's son really was a hindrance. I did not want a lifestyle that causes a person to be away from family as much as ministry did to my family. Yet I found myself on my knees surrendering to full-time ministry that day because I recognized the only thing that was holding me back was a faith issue, not a call issue.

So I have never viewed ministry as a job, career, or a place for advancement. I have discovered, and am still discovering, God's call is real. Serving him has become not what I do but who I am.

I tell you my story to allow you the opportunity to see if it may apply to your life's story. Are you working to make ends meet? Are you just busied and caught up in life? Are you connecting with what God wants you do accomplish? Whatever we do—ministry, housecleaning, stay-at-home parent, teacher, bus driver, etc.—it should be seen as a calling from God. We should be using the gifts God has given to us so we will find fulfillment yet more importantly discover how being called can make a difference in other people's lives. Thus, you become a living witness of the grace God has given to us through Jesus.

During this strange time that we are living through, we have an opportunity to discover anew what God is asking from us. "O ye of little faith!" (Matthew 8:26 NIV). Get up and change your life and become what God wants you to be. Serve him in whatever vocation you have chosen. Just be confident it is what God has called you to be and do.

Gracious loving Creator, enlighten us today with your call to living for you. Enable us to be seen as serving you, sharing you, in all we do. May our faith grow each day with the confidence that comes from our faithfulness. Amen.

Man, Was I in Trouble— Big Time Trouble!

t was a Wednesday night service at First Baptist Church of Greenville, South Carolina. My sister and I had cooked up a plan that we knew would get us in trouble, but we did not care. We were preacher's kids, you know. There was always a time for hymn requests during the service, so we waited patiently for the hymn "Love Lifted Me" by James Rowe. Someone seemingly always requested that hymn. About halfway through the hymns, someone requested it. We got ready. Ready to pounce on it. Here it came. You remember the words "I was sinking deep in sin, far from the peaceful shore …" When the congregation sang, "I was sinking deep in sin," we shouted out with joy, *"Yippee!"* so all could hear us! Then seeing our mother's face, our father's frown, the feeling came upon us *Oh my. We are in trouble.* Nowadays, I remember that exercise in futility every time the hymn is sung. I must admit I remember that mischievous plan with a little smile on my face.

I recalled that experience when I was reading Psalm 69. (The words "I sink in the miry depths" triggered the sinking deep in sin.) I must say that if you only read the first twenty-nine verses, it has to be one of the most depressing passages in all of scripture. It begins with these words: "Save me, O God, for the waters have come up to my neck. I sink in the miry depths, where there is no foothold. I have come into the deep waters; the floods engulf me. I am worn out calling for help; my throat is parched. My eyes fail, looking for my God" (Psalm 69:1–3 NIV). Talk about a person caught in the bog of sin and despair, sinking with no apparent hope. Then the honest voice of the psalmist, David himself, turns things around by saying, "I will praise God's name in song and glorify him with thanksgiving" (Psalm 69:30 NIV). The rest of the psalm is an absolute affirmation of God and what God will do for his people.

Hear what I have to say today, please. David, writing a hymn to be sung during worship in the temple of God located in Jerusalem, is demonstrating how we are to approach God in worship. Express our heartfelt despair, doubt, frustration, and fears, then turn our attitude toward what we all know God has done, is doing, and will do. Finish with an affirmation of trust and faith. God knows our thoughts, our fears, and our anxiety even before we began to open our mouths. He still wants us to open up and speak truth to him.

Have you ever been to a counselor, therapist, or psychiatrist? Isn't it the same principle in good therapy? Encourage the client to open up, be honest, and speak their truth. That is when healing begins, and only then will it begin. Is there a better therapist than God himself? Then we must be honest, open, and speak our truth! Yet have the faith to trust him. Is not that Jesus's way of praying to God? Read Luke 22:42.

> Oh God, our therapist and healer, our counselor, why are we having to go through a time like this? Why are so many people unemployed or furloughed? Why is our economy in such bad condition? We feel as if hope is running faster away from us than toward us. There is so much we do not understand. But we trust you. You see the big picture. We know there is a plan you will unfold before us. Revive us as your people, and enable us to be a part of the great renewal that you are about to bring. Allow us to live consistently with your will for us, rather than immersed in the confusion in this world. Amen.

Dipping into the Water of Strife/Quarreling/Testing; Been There Too Many Times!

Just thinking for a few minutes, really not very long, I came up with at least ten times in my life when I dipped into the spiritual waters wanting comfort from God only to find myself questioning God. Where is your cooling soothing water? Why God is your well dry? Why have you brought me here only to let me thirst for what I am not getting? Have I not learned enough? Why test me more?

Is this not the same thing that happened in Exodus 17:1–7 when the people of God, the Israelites, the chosen people, came to a place called Meribah? A portion reads, "There was no water for the people to drink. So they quarreled with Moses and said, 'Give us water to drink.' Moses replied, 'Why do you quarrel with me? Why do you put the Lord to the test?' But the people were thirsty for water there, and they grumbled against Moses. They said, 'Why did you bring us up out of Egypt to make us and our children and livestock die of thirst?' Then Moses cried out to the Lord, 'What am I to do with these people? They are almost ready to stone me" (Exodus 17:1–4 NIV). The people of God brought strife and quarreling before Moses, and because they were not happy with having to prove their faithfulness to God in challenging times, God was not pleased. It became a tragic moment in faith history that greatly disappointed God. How disappointed was God? When God was talking to Moses regarding the fact he was not going to go into the Promised Land with the people, God said, "This is because both of you (Moses and Aaron) broke faith with me in the presence of the Israelites at the waters of Meribah Kadesh in the Desert of Zin and because you did not uphold my holiness among the Israelites" (Deuteronomy 32:51 NIV).

The people were tested by God. Tested just the same way they were tested throughout the journey from slavery to promises. As in most situations, they failed the test. Yet God used all of these failures to shape his people. He wanted them to be worthy of what God was promising. He wanted them to work for what was about to be given them: God's grace, his free gift of salvation through forgiveness. All we have to do is *trust* him, even when we face a dry well. We prove our faithfulness regarding salvation through trusting our Heavenly Father in all circumstances and even in a crisis.

Look at two implications from this experience at Meribah. First is how God tests his people so they can show how much they trust God. Is this our hour of testing? Is this our moment to prove what we believe or our time to show our lack of faith? That's the choice we as individuals and as churches must face when all the world seems to be existing in chaos. Those who are trustworthy are the ones who are calm and know God is in control. We must be patient and focused, asking, "What is God about to do? Renewal?"

The second implication is for people like me, ministers—people God has called to lead his people toward his promises. We too can fail. Fail to "uphold God's holiness before his people." This is the burden of responsibility we carry with us throughout the wilderness times of life. When we become weak in our faith, that weakness causes the challenges like Meribah to become more than just a quarrel. It brings disgrace on the holiness of God. So I say to you today, standing on the mountaintop of God's Word, trust the one, the only one, who is worthy to be called holy! God himself! Do not show weakness during our Meribah time of testing! David says, "In your distress you called and I rescued you, I answered you out of a thundercloud; I tested you at the waters of Meribah" (Psalm 81:7 NIV).

God of Moses and Aaron, God of that testy group of Israelites, may we in our struggles trust you even when we feel the cool comforting waters of your well are dry. Help us to always know you will give us "Living Water" in your time. Amen.

Anticipation of the Promise

In the hot July heat of 1972, I drove from Birmingham to Beaumont, Texas, with an engagement ring. Becky and I had already decided to get married, but there was the responsibility in our minds, as old-fashioned as we were, to ask her parents for permission. I will not go into all the details of that experience, for lack of space in this devotion. However, I need you to know this. After all the joy, celebration, relief, and permission given, it was time to talk about setting the date. It went somewhat this way. Thanksgiving? No. Christmas? No. Spring break? No. Then I said, "OK, then when can we get married?" "Not until you graduate, Buddy." OK then. We set the date for June 1, 1973. I was planning to graduate May. However, what was not said was I was thinking of staying in school for another year. Oops! Guess that was a simple omission. What I want to point out by this story was we had a promise made to each other. We had a promise made by Becky's parents. We still had to wait a year. A year of anticipation of the promise.

Jeremiah 29:10–13 has Jeremiah proclaiming to the people of God God's promise.

> "I will come to you and fulfill my gracious promise to bring you back to this place. For I know the plans I have for you," declares the LORD, "plans to prosper you and not to harm you, plans to give you hope and a future. Then you will call upon me and come and pray to me, and I will listen to you. You will seek me and find me when you seek me with all your heart."

Oh yes. I left out a little phrase that might have an effect on this passage. Verse 10 begins, "When 70 years are completed in Babylon" (Jeremiah 29:10 NIV).

God's plan is great, yet it is hard to have patience with his timing. Seventy years! Good grief! Here we are today complaining about three months away from church! God must have a reason. There must be a plan in all this. Process with me. When you anticipate a promise, there is hope in what is to come. There is something to look forward to. Something that constantly draws us looking to the future for what is about to happen.

Lessons learned may be this. God has a plan for you, but we must accept his timetable. God will guide your life, but you have to be willing to follow. God will listen to you, but you must learn to talk to him. God gives you a future, but you must first believe. Do you comprehend this?

Paul says several things that help us understanding God's timing and promise. "Be joyful in hope, patient in affliction, faithful in prayer" (Romans 12:12 NIV). "But we also rejoice in our sufferings, because we know that suffering produces perseverance; perseverance, character; and character, hope. And hope does not disappoint us, because God has poured out his love into our hearts by the Holy Spirit, whom he has given us" (Romans 5:3–5 NIV). "But the fruit of the Spirit is love, joy, peace, patience, kindness, goodness, faithfulness, gentleness, and self-control. Against such things there is no law. Those who belong to Christ Jesus have crucified the sinful nature with its passions and desires" (Galatians 5:22–24 NIV). All seem to me to be words useful for us to have in our arsenal of faith while we anticipate God's promises: hope, patient, prayer, perseverance, character, love, and Holy Spirit. How are you doing during this period of anticipation of the promise? How about the anticipation of our eternal promises?

God of kept promises and enabler of anticipated promises to come, give us all the qualities we need to be your witnesses through our periods of waiting on the fulfillment of your promises. Let us be good stewards, found faithful, in keeping the truths associated with faith and trust. Amen.

See What These Five Words Will Do

You almost have to invent words to describe the experience. Words like *awesome, awe-inspiring, emotional,* and *life-changing* do not even come close. I am talking about December 29, 1974. This was the day I was ordained. I have the photograph in front of me now. Each person in the photo had a wonderful influence in my life. The ordination service was unique in many ways. One special aspect was in the fact that it was a rare joint service of the First Baptist Church of Birmingham and the Mountain Brook Baptist Church. I grew up in Mountain Brook and had served as a youth minister at FBC. My father's ordination message outline was captured in a cross-stitch done by my sister Carol Lois Stevens. These thoughts were framed and are on my bedroom wall, so I see them every morning. Reminders of the challenge given, and the kind of minister I strive to become. It simply says, "Be yourself; Be honest; Be compassionate; Be loving; Be determined; and Be a child of God." These are words worthy of becoming guideposts for anyone trying to live worthy of being a Christ follower, especially for those of us who feel called to full-time Christian service. Words masterfully constructed can have a powerful influence.

Look with me to the psalms today. Psalm 37 is one I stumbled across in looking for what to convey in today's devotion. Verses 1–11 seem vital for us on this day. "Do not fret because of evil men or be envious of those who do wrong; for like the grass they will soon wither, like green plants they will soon die away" (Psalm 37:1–2 NIV). "For evil men will be cut off, but those who hope in the Lord will inherit the land. A little while, and the wicked will be no more; though you look for them, they will not be found" (Psalm 37:9–10 NIV). Do you see how verses 1–2 and 9–10 talk about "evil men"?

David appeals for God's people to see how to traverse through evil in the world by saying, "Do not fret ... They will be cut off" (Psalm 37:1 NIV). These thoughts in verses 1–2 and 9–10 are the bookends of five words that should become the volumes of our lives. "Trust in the LORD and do good; dwell in the land and enjoy safe pasture. Delight yourself in the LORD and he will give you the desires of your heart. Commit your way to the LORD; trust in him and he will do this: He will make your righteousness shine like the dawn, the justice of your cause like the noonday sun. Be still before the LORD and wait patiently for him; do not fret when men succeed in their ways, when they carry out their wicked schemes. Refrain from anger and turn from wrath; do not fret—it leads only to evil (Psalm 37:3–8 NIV). Look at these verses closely. You will discover these five terms: *trust, delight, commit, be still,* and *refrain.* Frame them on the walls of your heart and make them your guides for living. Especially when there is evil around you. Now look at the five terms from Psalm 37:3–8.

No matter what anyone else is doing, "trust god and do good." Do not be influenced by events or others; be the one influencing others in a positive way. "delight" or find joy in God's loving presence each and every moment. How can fear overtake us when we are, pardon the reference but it fits, dancing with joy in the presence of our Holy God? Joy is always there to be discovered; we simply need to open the doors or our hearts. "Commit" your way to the Lord. Commit means you are determined to stick to the plan that he has laid out. Do not jump off the track. Stay focused. Evil wants us to look backward, which leads to disaster. "Be still and wait patiently." This is the most difficult part of being a trustworthy believer. We are a society that wants the quick fix. We want a pat on the back and the feeling all is OK. Grow up! You know the best things in life are those things that are worth waiting for. How can we know God if we do not stay still and trust him? Finally, "refrain from anger." In sports, if you allow your opponent to make you angry, they win. Keep cool, keep calm, and keep on the track of faithful service.

Trust, delight, commit, be still, and *refrain.* See what these five terms will do for your life of faith. Write them down and read them over and over throughout the day. They will make a difference!

> God, you gave us these words. May we follow them confidently without fear. Amen.

Finish the Game: Practice and Determination

A man who influenced my life probably more than my own family, at a time I truly needed a positive influence, was Darrell Fitts. He came into my life when he arrived as the new head football coach at my high school. He was additionally the assistant principal. This meant he was in charge of discipline. Oh, the stories he can tell. I will not share his phone number with you! Coach Fitts believed in teaching us every aspect of the sport. He wanted us all to know the whys and hows of what we were doing. One humorous moment was when we were playing our first game with him as our coach. He came into the locker room and saw how ridiculous we looked dressing. It was as if no one knew how to put on our new game uniforms. I can still hear his voice. "You may not play like all-Americans, but by God, you will look like it when you go onto the field." Another thing that had an effect on me was his belief in practicing so hard and going over the game plan so many times that it became second nature. "You have to have the determination to play hard and finish the game without overthinking." Practice, determination, hard work, and finish the game. Rules to live by.

In Hebrews 10:19–25, we find some very insightful ideas that need to germinate in our minds. The first four verses are basically saying to us that because of what Jesus has done for us and the freedom we have as Christ followers, there are some things we need to pursue. "Let us hold unswervingly to the hope we profess, for he who promised is faithful" (Hebrews 10:23 NIV). Have the determination to hold on to the faith you have found in Christ. Do not allow anyone or anything to pull you away.

Stick to God's game plan, no matter what. This, people, takes practice so that we know God's plan so well that we are not overthinking. It takes hard work daily to be ready for the difficult times to finish the game of life.

"And let us consider how we may spur one another on toward love and good deeds" (Hebrews 10:24 NIV). When we accept Christ as our hope, our joy, and our provider of forgiveness, we also accept our fellow believers as our encouragers and our responsibility. Have you ever thought about it that way? Two sides of the coin of relationships. You need to if you have not. We need each other. The church, the body of believers who make up the church, needs each person who is a part of that family of faith to care enough about each other to encourage each other. When life knocks us down, our faith family should be there to give us a hand up. Being a believer is not all about what you get; it is equally about how much you must give. It is all based on what we have in common: Christ. All other differences should be set aside when it comes to faith family. It may not be that way all the time, but it should be.

"Let us not give up meeting together, as some are in the habit of doing, but let us encourage one another" (Hebrews 10:25 NIV). The early church began with meeting in synagogues and the temple. It then had to shift to meeting in homes. Later it shifted in some places like Rome to the catacombs. Once Christianity became legal, buildings were built. Today we are discovering that we can assemble though technology. Do you know what encourages me? Seeing the comments, likes, shares, and participation. We are still together and have added multitudes to our devotions and broadcasts. It keeps us in the game of life as faith believers and as witnesses. We—no matter the difficulty of life's challenges, the controversies of public events, or how we feel physically, mentally, or spiritually—need to stay focused on finishing the game, encouraging each other. Practice, determination, and hard work will get us there. Will you pay the price for success as a believer?

Holy Comforter, challenge us today to be encouragers and participants in your game plan. Amen.

Do We Get It Wrong? Maybe, so It's Time to Think

When I was a struggling teenager, trying to figure out who I was and wanting to be a better person and Christian, there was a revival at my home church. Dr. Paul Stevens was preaching. He was at the time the head of the Southern Baptist Convention Radio and Television Commission—a pioneer in Southern Baptist broadcasting. I do not remember what he preached, how long he preached, or anything else about the service, but like it was yesterday, I remember feeling the only thing I could do was to walk the aisle and rededicate my life. My mother was so proud. My father felt, I am sure, maybe there was hope for this boy after all. It was a refreshing, emotional, joyous moment in my life. I would say it was as real as anything I have experienced. Fast-forward six months. I was right back where I was prior to that life-changing moment. Why, God, can't I get it right?

Years later, when I began to really study God's Word, I found a new best friend in Paul. Still my hero! He was not with Jesus during his earthly ministry, yet he encountered him and his life was changed. He writes as someone who is like us, trying to work through all the significance of Jesus and his teachings. He makes Jesus's teachings and life understandable to folks like us. Maybe Jesus was thinking about Paul, or at least people like Paul, when Jesus said, "Then Jesus told him, 'Because you have seen me, you have believed; blessed are those who have not seen and yet have believed'" (John 20:29 NIV). Why do I call Paul my hero? Look at 1 Timothy 1:15 with me today. "Here is a trustworthy saying that deserves full acceptance: Christ Jesus came into the world to save sinners—of whom I am the worst" (1 Timothy 1:15 NIV).

Was Paul considering himself the worst sinner because he was a blasphemer, persecutor, and violent? Was he the worst sinner because he lacked proper perspective as to what God was doing in Christ? Was he the worst sinner because he failed in the past to do better? I have discovered another way of looking at Paul's overwhelming sense of sin. Just look at the last six words above in verse 15. "Of whom I am the worst." In Greek, the word is *ego*. It is the emphatic first-person pronoun. *I am*! It is not *I was*. It is not *I might be*. It is not *someone made me do it*. It is clearly *I am*! Here is where Paul and I connect so well. Right now, after forty-eight years in the ministry, I must say in all honesty I am, or I am still, a sinner. Saved by grace, yes, but I am a sinner. Every day in this world I struggle to be what God chooses for me to be. If we ever lose sight of this idea and feel we are perfect and nothing else needs to be addressed in our lives, we fail our midterms. We are sinners! Get it! This is who we are. Sinners saved by grace!

When God calls us to accept Jesus, he is not wanting us to wait until we have perfected our lives. He calls out to us to begin the process of pursuing perfection, just as we are. He loves us, continues to forgive us, guides us, encourages us, and gives us his Holy Spirit to comfort us. The first step of accepting Jesus is the most important one. You cannot move forward until you take that first step. Yet that is just the beginning. Paul says, "Christ Jesus came into the world to save sinners" (1 Timothy 1:15 NIV). Acknowledge you are a sinner. Continue to acknowledge you are a sinner, but a sinner walking with Jesus. Then the world of faith begins to open up for you, and life will reach toward perfection.

Father of our Savior Jesus Christ, forgive us each day, just as you give us our daily bread. Love us even at our worst and empower us to strive for the best you have to offer. Make life easier to live through your love and devotion toward us. May we be as devoted toward you and others. Amen.

Old Thoughts; New Songs

The year was 1998. It began with an overwhelming shock that went through our family, and instead of getting better or even just easing a bit, it only seemed to get worse. It was an emotional roller coaster running out of control. In January my sister, Mary Grace, died after suffering in the hospital for two months with cancer. Then late in May, my father took a turn and was hospitalized. His mental and physical deterioration had finally caught up with him. We were very aware his life here on the earth with us was coming to a close. Finally, the doctor came into the room and informed me that the hospital could no longer keep him there and we needed to make arrangements. The choice, which no family wants to make, had to be made. We admitted him to a nursing home. The one blessing in all of this was he was no longer aware of where he was. While there in the nursing home, an interesting development occurred. First the chaplain, then a nurse, stopped me on a visit and said, "Just stand outside his room for a few minutes before you go in." Curious to discover this secret they wanted me to find, I stood there. Then I heard a most remarkable thing. My father, who was not known as a singer, was singing hymn after hymn. They said this was going on the entire day while he was awake. He might not have recognized me, or known where he was, but he was singing the old hymns as if he was preparing for the heavenly chorus. It was rehearsal time!

I find it interesting how the Bible talks about the joy of singing. "Speak to one another with psalms, hymns, and spiritual songs. Sing and make music in your heart to the Lord, always giving thanks to God the Father for everything, in the name of our Lord Jesus Christ" (Ephesians 5:19–20 NIV). Then in the Old Testament there are six psalms and Isaiah 42:10

where we read about singing new songs. In the New Testament, we read in the book of Revelation, "And they sang a new song: 'You are worthy to take the scroll and to open its seals, because you were slain, and with your blood you purchased men for God from every tribe and language and people and nation'" (Revelation 5:9 NIV). "And they sang a new song before the throne and before the four living creatures and the elders" (Revelation 14:3 (NIV).

I have never understood the divide that occurs among believers over the joy of singing. "Is it the old hymns? Is it the new praise songs? You choose!" If this is our attitude, then you tell me what is Christian about that kind of attitude? Where is putting others first, loving one another, and seeking the highest possible good? There is such a great joy of faith expressed in many of the newer Christian songs. A joy that should never be suppressed by us who grew up with a different style of music. There is so much comfort that comes into our hearts when we hear the old songs that have been around for a long time. Yet God is still revealing new ways to express this joy in new songs also. I want to see a miracle take place in churches today where the younger folks and the older folks can join hands and sing each other's songs of faith. Having a real blend of sounds, generations, joy, and worship. As Christ followers, can we not compromise and walk through life together expressing ourselves in unity, even as we blend our hearts, joy, and songs into a harmonious spiritual experience? That would almost be like heaven! I guess that is what I want us to have: heavenly joy.

Just remember when we arrive at the gates of heaven, we will not be asked what songs we will sing. We are not in charge. If life is a preparation for heaven, we'd better start doing a better job of getting along.

> *Father of all creation, enlighten our hearts today with such a joy we sing praises to you. Enable us to remember we all have different ways to express our praise and joy. Let us not dampen the joy of others by selfish desires. Your will be done on earth as we will sing in heaven. Amen.*

Lions, Fires, and Crisis

We had rules. Strict rules. Rules that were to help us conform, behave, and act responsibly. I never liked rules. In my way of thinking, rules were meant to be broken. If you could break a rule and get away with it, then life was good. What I learned was this: rules were also like spotlights. They enabled the rule givers, parents, to know when you had stepped over the line. Invisible bells, bells unheard by the rule breaker, would ring in their ears, "He's doing it again." Yes, I am saying I usually got caught. Now the rule about getting caught was "Because you have disappointed us, we are pulling in the fences. As you prove yourself worthy, we will once again expand the fences and allow you to do more of the things you want to do with your friends." (Fancy way of saying, "You are grounded until you prove you are responsible.") I learned a lot about proving I could be responsible. How do you prove you are responsible?

In Daniel 6, we learn about Daniel proving he was responsible to God above King Darius. The tricksters and jealous crowd of rulers went to King Darius and enticed him to make a decree that no one could pray to any god or man during a thirty-day period. They knew Daniel would be faithful in prayer to his God. They knew this would break the relationship between the king and Daniel. Faced with a choice of being responsible and faithful, Daniel prayed anyway. Crisis! Daniel was taken by the lies of a den of liars and thrown into a den of lions. When God protected him and King Darius saw what God had done for Daniel, the scripture says, "The king was overjoyed and gave orders to lift Daniel out of the den. And when Daniel was lifted from the den, no wound was found on him, because he had trusted in his God" (Daniel 6:23 NIV). In a crisis, he was protected by God because he was responsible and faithful. He did not allow a crisis to shake his faith.

In Daniel 3, we learn about Shadrach, Meshach, and Abednego proving their responsibility to God above an idol. King Nebuchadnezzar had a golden image of himself built and commanded that all people were to bow down and worship this image. Our three heroes refused and were thrown into the fiery furnace. Crisis! When they came out unhindered, scripture says, "Then Nebuchadnezzar said, 'Praise be to the God of Shadrach, Meshach and Abednego, who has sent his angel and rescued his servants! They trusted in him and defied the king's command and were willing to give up their lives rather than serve or worship any god except their own God" (Daniel 3:28 NIV). In a crisis, they were responsible and faithful.

When I was faced with the crisis of learning to grow up, my parents taught the value of acting responsibly. When Daniel faced a crisis, he proved his responsibility and his faithfulness. This influenced a nation. When Shadrach, Meshach, and Abednego faced a crisis of life and death, they were able to influence a powerful ruler.

We are facing our own crisis of life, faith, trust, growing up spiritually, and being responsible. How are we doing? Are we showing spiritual maturity? Are we, by our faithfulness, proving the power of God over our weaknesses? Are we influencing others positively? In the crisis of a pandemic or any other crisis, it is time for God's people to accept the challenge of acting responsibly and demonstrating our faithfulness to God. Prove there is no one or nothing that can distract us from our faith. Be a solution finder, not a problem maker. Be a comfort giver, not an insecurity instigator. Be a prayer warrior, not a conspiracy spreader. Let us be a people of faith, proving in our time of crisis that we are responsible and faithful.

God, we know you have called us to be faithful in all situations. Help us to filter the noise and find your truth. Let the world find you through our responsibility and faithfulness. Amen.

Gloom, Despair, Agony, and God's Grace

s there a movie you watch over and over again where you can almost say the words with the actors? One of my favorite quotes was in *McClintock* when Chill Wills wanted to get the attention of the crowd. He would stand and declare, "People, people, people." Then there are shows on television with a silly piece of music that becomes so lodged in your brain cells that you will never be able to release it. One such piece of music was on the weekly show *Hee Haw* (1969–1992) when Roy Clark and Buck Owens would sing, "Gloom, despair, and agony on me. Deep, dark depression, excessive misery. If it weren't for bad luck, I'd have no luck at all. Gloom, despair, and agony on me." I bet you began to sing it as you read it.

We have to choose how we want to approach life. Yes, I said choose! Circumstances that come our way do not determine our outlook on life. It truly is how we choose to face those circumstances. Life can be out of control, but we can choose not to be out of control. It is my experience that the beautiful, undeniable, still small voice of God himself resonates in our ears most when we are in the midst of the most uncontrollable circumstances. It is as if his actions demonstrate to us a nonverbal declaration *OK, now that I have your attention, listen to what I want you to hear from me.* The Bible is full of thoughts and ideas that are there for us to discover. All of which will bring comfort and understanding. I did a search of the phrase *all things* this morning. Wow! All things are under his control. Look up these few I have listed today: John 1:3, Romans 8:37, 2 Corinthians 4:15, and 1 Peter 4:11.

I want to point out for this devotional two of the comments Paul expressed.

"I can do everything through him who gives me strength" (Philippians 4:13 NIV).

"To keep me from becoming conceited because of these surpassingly great revelations, there was given me a thorn in my flesh, a messenger of Satan, to torment me" (2 Corinthians 12:7 NIV)

Both comments are lights guiding our attitudes in life.

These two passages have been my personal emotional and spiritual crutch through the past fifty years. I have held on tightly to them, because they are my daily reminder of the choice we make in dealing with all we are challenged to face in life. So "people, people, people," listen to what I am saying. In dealing with the daily consequences related to severe back pain for fifty years, I have discovered a small glimpse of the passing glory of God's grace, which is more than sufficient. Life is more enjoyable, more desirable, and more fulfilling when we discover the awesome power of God's grace. There is no room left for gloom, despair, and agony. I choose God's grace. Will you? I really wish I did not need to face my third surgery on my lower back on July 9. However, I know there is a lesson to be learned, and God's grace will be more than sufficient. I never like talking about my personal health issues because I do not want them to be a distraction. However, it is my prayer that someone can learn from my experience, like Paul's thorn, how we face life truly is a choice. Choose God's grace! Please! It really does give us a brighter outlook on life.

God of healing and strength, give us today an extra measure of your grace so we can all see how you give us the strength to face all challenges. Amen.

The World Turned Upside Down within Two Decades

So many life events have taken place in the last twenty-one years since September 11, 2001. Our world has changed forever. It will never be the same. The question is this: what will we do to make our world a better place?

Let us journey back to the world of the early church. Rome was in power. In the years following the death and resurrection of Jesus, so many events altered the Roman world forever. Let us jump twenty-one years after the earthly ministry of Jesus. The early churches were struggling to survive and struggling even more to maintain the purity of the gospel they had been called to spread into the world. This is evident in Paul's writing, especially his letters to the church at Corinth. Then Nero was proclaimed emperor of Rome from AD 54 to 68. In AD 64, he set fire to the inner city of Rome so he could build his planned palatial complex called Domus Aurea (Golden House). He avoided taking the blame by blaming the Christians, thus starting the persecution of all Christians in the empire. During this same period, the Jews in Israel revolted against Rome from AD 66 to 74. The temple in Jerusalem was destroyed, and Jerusalem itself was flattened in AD 70. This revolt was finally ended in AD 74 with the fall of Masada where 960 Jews committed suicide to avoid being taken as slaves. Then on top of these world-changing events, Mount Vesuvius erupted, burying Pompeii and other areas in AD 79. The world was in chaos.

We think we have it bad today. History tells us not really. Not compared to other world-changing times in the past. It is not what happens to us that is the issue. It is how we deal with the circumstances that come our way. It is how God's church, God's people, and God's plan are used in challenging times to proclaim hope, peace, joy, and love to a world that is desperately seeking just what we have to offer to them. Get up, church of God, and do what we were called to accomplish!

Revelation, written following the destruction of Jerusalem in AD 70 and following all of the events above mentioned earlier, is the proclamation of Jesus to John, a prisoner on the Island of Patmos. John recorded this. "When I saw him, I fell at his feet as though dead. Then he placed his right hand on me and said: 'Do not be afraid. I am the First and the Last. I am the Living One; I was dead, and behold I am alive for ever and ever! And I hold the keys of death and Hades.'" (Revelation 1:17 NIV). That's it! The message we need in desperate times! We need to feel his comforting hand placed on our shoulder and feel the reassurance that he is in control. He is always with us and advocating for us. What then shall we fear?

If his message was good enough 1,940 years ago, it is good enough now. Especially since we see how his message of hope has stood the test of time.

> *God of all of creation who holds the future in your hands, give us peace in the midst of the storm, and give us your strength to be your witnesses in troubled times. Amen.*

What You Want, You Cannot Have: Temptation

When my mother was entertaining special guests, her wonderful treat for dessert was to make a four- to six-inch flat, crispy meringue base, put a scoop of ice cream on top, and then top that with a fresh, juicy, homemade strawberry sauce on top. I loved that dessert. But no, it was too much trouble to make just for us. Only when special guests came did we have that dessert. The meringue base was the hard part. It had to be made days ahead, and the humidity had to be low or the meringue would be chewy rather than the crispy texture that mother desired. They had to be perfect! Well, let me tell you what happened. They were so rare, I liked to sneak a meringue or two when I knew they were prepared. Mother would say, "What you want, you cannot have." In her thoughts, she was saying, *Do not be tempted.* In my mind, I heard her present me with a dare. One weekend we were entertaining Dr. F. Townley Lord, former president of the Baptist World Alliance. He was visiting from England. Mother found a new hiding place so I could not find the meringues. She had placed them in the oven, knowing I would not look there. I did not find them. However, she forgot and preheated the oven for supper, and yes, they were ruined. I could not convince her that I did nothing this time. But as she said when sending me to my room, "Your temptation caused me to ruin the evening!"

Temptations do ruin things for us and for the people we love. We find the story of the temptation in the Garden of Eden, Jesus was tempted prior to his ministry, Peter was tempted in the courtyard of the high priest, and we are tempted every day. We have this image of Satan in our minds as a snake tempting Adam and Eve, maybe Dante's image of a horned, red beast with a long tail, or even a movie-generated image of horror. In my mind's eye, I have an image that is even more fearful than any illustration you might have drummed up in your mind. Do you remember the temptations of Jesus? Satan was trying to cause Jesus to stumble and sidetrack him from what he was sent to do. "Jesus said to him, 'Away from me, Satan! For it is written: Worship the Lord your God and serve him only'" (Matthew 4:10 NIV). Jesus overcame and showed us that with God's help we can overcome temptation also. We find another moment of temptation. This is where I began to build my fear of Satan. The verse says, "Jesus turned and said to Peter, 'Get behind me, Satan! You are a stumbling block to me; you do not have in mind the things of God, but the things of men'" (Matthew 16:23 NIV).

So here is my most horror-filled image of Satan. It is not the sneaky snake or the devil made me do it concept. It is when good godly people like the strong Peter, the Rock, the one chosen to lead the church, keep from being focused on godly things and cause others to focus on worldly things. It is when good Christians like you and me cause others to stumble. When we become an impediment to others who are seeking truth and needing God, that is when Satan wins his greatest victories. That is pure evil. That is the way Satan works. That is when the fires of hell are the hottest.

> God of wisdom and truth, you said through your servant Paul, "Do not be overcome by evil, but overcome evil with good." May we be determined to be overcomers and not be used by Satan for his nasty deeds. Let us be lights illuminating the way to Jesus. Amen.

Let's Make a Quick Stop

I t was getting late in the afternoon, and I was not sure we would be able to go in. Let's make a quick stop and just see. The sign said all tours end at 5 p.m. It was right at 5, but let's try. We were in Richmond, Virginia. Becky was there for a missions meeting. I went along on the trip and we took a few more days for a vacation. There were so many sights to see. History was everywhere we looked. This quick stop was different. It was St. John's Episcopal Church. I wanted to see the reserved box where Patrick Henry and his family sat to worship, back in the colonial and revolutionary days. The man was closing the doors when we arrived. "Sorry, folks. The tours are over." I put on the saddest eyes I could muster and told him how much I just wanted to see the place where Patrick Henry sat, then we would leave. He let us in and walked us to the spot on the left side near the front of the sanctuary. There it was. The man from the church said quietly, "I know you asked about where Mr. Henry sat, but we prefer to say this is where he stood." I understood completely. Standing on this very spot, on March 23, 1775, at a meeting of the Second Virginia Convention, Patrick Henry gave his memorable speech "Give Me Liberty or Give Me Death." One of the great battle cries that changed the world. It was a quick stop to fulfill a dream. I stood where Patrick Henry stood.

We are approaching the Fourth of July celebration. It is just eight days away. It will be the 244th year, as of this devotion being written, that we have celebrated the independence of our nation. I want you to take a quick stop for this devotion and contemplate where you stand today. Upon what principles are you willing to say you will die?

I, as just one voice, believe the greatest hope, truth, and guiding principle for America today is to rediscover the power of God's Word.

We need to allow it once again to permeate all we do and influence all we desire as Americans. There has been too much diluting of the scriptures for personal gain and using it for wrong reasons. I want to stand for the purity of the sacred words from God as they speak for themselves. I do not feel they need defending. I believe they simply need proclaiming. Truth is truth and worth dying for. Millions have.

Let's make a quick stop, as an example. "Be joyful always; pray continually; give thanks in all circumstances, for this is God's will for you in Christ Jesus. Do not put out the Spirit's fire; do not treat prophecies with contempt. Test everything. Hold on to the good. Avoid every kind of evil" (1 Thessalonians 5:16–22 NIV). Always, in all of the craziness of our day. Always, when no one knows who to listen to. Always, when we are frightened, confused, and want to run away from everything. Always, there is the voice of God that creates a positive outlook when we listen. These are just a few words that guide us when we take the time to mute the roar of society. Do you hear them? Listen to God and his Holy Word.

Get it? Just take a quick stop with God's guiding words, and you will find the calming definition as to how to live today. The preacher does not need to tell you what it means. A preacher can only guide you to discover for yourself what scriptures mean for your lives. They speak for themselves.

God, the Word from the beginning of time, give us your hope, your truth, and your guidance for today so we can live differently, with a positive outlook, even in times when there is no normal. Amen.

What Are You Doing?

Yesterday morning began just like any other day. Routine. Then suddenly my thoughts came from some strange corner of my brain. *What are you doing?* That is what I asked myself. Here I was, standing in front of the mirror, shaving cream on my face, the sharpest item in my house in my hand, ready to shave. *What are you doing?* I asked myself again. *When you are on the computer, you wear glasses. When you want to read, you wear glasses. When you drive, Buddy, you wear glasses. Here you are about to shave with a five-blade razor coming toward your jugular, and you can barely see. What are you doing?* Well, it is really hard to shave wearing glasses. I had a laugh and went on. It is all about image, isn't it? We want to look good and will do what it takes to groom ourselves properly. Well, most of us do. There are days I have this beastly desire to not shave, to not brush my hair, and to wear sandals, shorts, and a T-shirt to preach. Never have given in to that desire. I worry about how people perceive what I look like.

I can remember trying on a new suit at the old Eastwood Mall. I looked in the mirror to see how it fit, but my focus was not on the suit. Rather, I saw how much my hair was receding and how the scars on the top of my head showed. I panicked. I do not want people to see my scars! My anxiety went up. I did not buy the suit, but I went to my barber who sold me some expensive shampoo, guaranteed to help hair grow. It did not work; you can tell. What was I thinking?

We spend large amounts of money to try to enhance our image. We are so very concerned about how people perceive us that we become consumers of products that promise to make us look like movie stars and magazine models. Our society is so image conscious that we now have medical professionals who deal with the crisis of eating disorders, doctors who specialize in surgery to alter our physical appearance, and over-the-counter medications for just about anything. We are rapidly becoming obsessed more with what others think we look like on the outside than what others see in us. What are we doing?

The Bible takes a different approach to what is important in life. God is more concerned with who we are than what we look like. We can cover up most anything with clothes, makeup, and surgery. We cannot hide who we really are. I think that is what we find in these words: "But the fruit of the Spirit is love, joy, peace, patience, kindness, goodness, faithfulness, gentleness, and self-control. Against such things there is no law. Those who belong to Christ Jesus have crucified the sinful nature with its passions and desires. Since we live by the Spirit, let us keep in step with the Spirit. Let us not become conceited, provoking and envying each other" (Galatians 5:22–26 NIV).

Think with me today about what is important. Is it not more important to be a godly person than it is to try to adjust your image to be something you think others will like? God wants us to be changed from within. He wants us to be filled so full of his spirit that other people overlook our outward appearance and see the fruits of what God has done in us. It is called personality and character that make you who you are! Let Jesus come into your heart and be who God has created you to be through faith.

God of all creation, enable us to be conscious of our inner-self and not so consumed with our outward appearance. Enable us to be more concerned about what you see in us than we are with how we think other people perceive us. Enable us to understand how our faith-filled life is the most important aspect of who we are. Amen.

It Is Time!

Yes, it is time for us to put life in proper perspective. It is time for us to get a grip on the issues of our day. It is time for us to slow down and prioritize, synthesize, organize, and understand, with all the myths, half truths, lies, and confusion that are added to all the distractions, smoke and mirrors, and misdirection, what really is factual. Do I have your attention now? Well, here goes. It is simple yet complex. It is easy yet challenging. It is right, but few do it. It is said in every generation, yet we never learn. It is true, yet we choose not to hear it.

When a person chooses to confess their sins, accept Jesus Christ as their Savior, acknowledge God sent his Son to die on the cross for our sins, and believe he was buried, rose on the third day, and was resurrected as the demonstration of the eternal life given to us, we become Christ followers. Then here it is, people! We as Christ followers are to rise above the challenges, problems, politics, and hatred in this world to become a reflection of the love of God we have found in Jesus Christ. Our primary function as believers is to praise God. It is not our place to be "carried away with every wind of doctrine" (Ephesians 4:14 NIV). Our purpose is to be his witnesses everywhere we go. Please read the following psalm three times while you are reading this devotion. It is time to stop blaming and start *praising* God. It is time to stop being like everyone else and start *praising* God. It is time to do and to be what God wants us to be so the world will become what he wants it to become.

> Praise the Lord. Praise the Lord, O my soul. I will praise the Lord all my life; I will sing praise to my God as long as I live. Do not put your trust in princes, in mortal men,

who cannot save. When their spirit departs, they return to the ground; on that very day their plans come to nothing. Blessed is he whose help is the God of Jacob, whose hope is in the Lord his God, the Maker of heaven and earth, the sea, and everything in them—the Lord, who remains faithful forever. He upholds the cause of the oppressed and gives food to the hungry. The Lord sets prisoners free, the Lord gives sight to the blind, the Lord lifts up those who are bowed down, the Lord loves the righteous. The Lord watches over the alien and sustains the fatherless and the widow, but he frustrates the ways of the wicked. The Lord reigns forever, your God, O Zion, for all generations. Praise the Lord. (Psalm 146:1–10 NIV)

We focus our attention on God because of his *help*, his *hope*, his *heaven*, and his *healing*. It is time to rise above the world so all people can see the difference Christ makes in the lives of his followers. Be the city on the hill (Matthew 5:14 NIV) praising and worshiping God with all of your energy. There is not a single issue or challenge too big for God. There are times when God needs his people to be bigger in our faith. The time is now!

Creator of the universe, you who gave us life for times like this, we humbly repent for our lack of faith when the world needs it the most. Restore within us a burning desire for renewal of your people so there can be revival in our land. Amen.

Frozen or Chosen

When I was in elementary school, one thing that I absolutely despised was when we decided to play a game of basketball, football, or baseball and someone would say, "Let's choose up sides." It seemed to most of the guys to be the fairest way of selecting a team. The two best players would select one right after the other. If there was not an even number of players, the last person was left out. That was usually me. "Oh, come on, Buddy. You can be with us." Unwanted, but fitted into the game. On the bench, but there. I felt, due to my lack of athletic abilities at that age, as if I were frozen out rather than being chosen to add value to the team. Now that I am writing this, I really did not despise it; I absolutely hated it. What it did for me, however, was create a determination to become a better player and prove to all the guys how wrong they were. I guess one could say being frozen out motivated me to become one who was chosen.

Remember Paul's words?

> Therefore, as God's chosen people, holy and dearly loved, clothe yourselves with compassion, kindness, humility, gentleness and patience. Bear with each other and forgive whatever grievances you may have against one another. Forgive as the Lord forgave you. And over all these virtues put on love, which binds them all together in perfect unity. Let the peace of Christ rule in your hearts, since as members of one body you were called to peace. And be thankful. Let the word of Christ dwell in you richly as you teach and admonish one another with all wisdom, and as

you sing psalms, hymns and spiritual songs with gratitude in your hearts to God. And whatever you do, whether in word or deed, do it all in the name of the Lord Jesus, giving thanks to God the Father through him. (Colossians 3:12–17 NIV)

Can you visualize the beauty of God's Word here? We are God's chosen! We are holy in his eyes! We are loved and appreciated! So this is how we are to present ourselves to the world. We are not to be frozen in a stagnant understanding of faith. Our faith is a living faith. We are refreshed in the living waters (John 4:10 NIV) and live as truly blessed followers of Christ. It is our compassion, kindness, humility, gentleness, and patience that show we understand what it is to be on God's team, worthy of being chosen. Read the rest of the passage again.

I challenge each of us to become motivated to learn more, practice more, pray more, and care more so we will be found faithful enough, and talented enough, to be on God's team. What the world needs now is love. The time is just right to play in the biggest game of our lives. Show the world what happens when we grow in our faith to point out the way we live can change the world. Let others see the light of Christ when we talk about the challenges of the day, post on Facebook, and even encounter those whose views are polar opposite from ours. Read the passage again. Does your faith show through sufficiently enough to be chosen?

God, you have loved us long before we were worthy of that love. You have challenged us to grow in our knowledge and faith. We pray today that you will choose us to be on your team as we begin to change this world for you. Amen.

It Is Something You Do!

I believe until this day it was one of my father's plans to guide my life without appearing to tell me what to do. He knew if he told me, I would not listen to the truths he wanted to share. You know how teenagers are. Our ability to reason is solidly protected by a steel, reinforced brick wall of stubbornness. He simply said something like "Buddy, Mrs. Garvin needs someone strong to help her carry some food to people in need. Would you be interested in helping?" Sure. I was strong, and I would be needed. That would be a great opportunity.

Growing up in Mountain Brook, Alabama, had not really given me very many times to see what poverty was like. Mrs. Garvin drove this young man out into the country, down dirt roads, and I saw what every person should see at some point in their lives. A family of five living in a one-room house with a dirt floor. The horn on the car honked, and all five knew the car and came running with total joy on their filthy faces. The food, the clothes, and the candy were much more appreciated than any Christmas gift I had ever received. I saw expressions of absolute joy, while Mrs. Garvin allowed tears to run down her face as she was so glad to have shared just a little. I witnessed in that very moment something I needed to see. Christian love in action. Faith is not just believing in Jesus; it becomes what you do because you believe in Jesus and understand his teachings.

Over the past forty-six years, since I was ordained, my attention keeps being drawn back to Paul's letter to the church at Rome. "Therefore, I urge you, brothers, in view of God's mercy, to offer your bodies as living sacrifices, holy and pleasing to God—this is your spiritual act of worship. Do not conform any longer to the pattern of this world, but be transformed by the renewing of your mind. Then you will be able to test and approve what God's will is—his good, pleasing and perfect will" (Romans 12:1–2 NIV). Allow me to paraphrase it in my way of thinking. Because of what God has done for you, worship him by doing what is right in his eyes. You are his witnesses by the way you live. Do not be a distraction. Show your love and appreciation by what you do each day. Do not be like others; be special. Then you will know God's will by the reaction of people you serve.

We live in a world that is facing challenges and is feeling overwhelmed. It is so easy to want to blame others for our problems or even develop dislike for anyone who disagrees with us. So I ask you this question: what do you think is God's will for us today? His good, pleasing, and perfect will? (Romans 12:1–2 NIV). Are we to join in believing and passing on conspiracy theories? Picking sides in every debate? Becoming involved in secular movements? Or do you believe God wants us to bring his love, his peace, his presence with us wherever we go? There are families going hungry. There are children depressed by what they have witnessed this year. There are teachers who do not know how the school year will proceed. There are churches changed forever due to the shutdown. How have you shown Christian love through your actions? How have you taken your faith and allowed it to become what you do because you believe in Jesus? We have been allowed to be here in this world for a time just like this. It is our time to shine brightly as followers of Christ!

Father who taught us Jesus is the light of the world, let this little light of mine shine, shine, shine! All around the neighborhood, let it shine. I will not hide it under a bushel; I will not allow Satan to put it out. Let it shine; let it shine; let it shine. Let my light shine so the world will be illuminated by Jesus through what I do. Amen.

Lessons Learned the Hard Way

His name was Mark. He was not very big. You could even call him frail. We all wondered why in the world he was trying to play football. He was slow and could not keep up with the rest of us. He was teased, and jokes were hurled his way. He even caused us to be punished on one occasion. We were running forty-yard dashes for conditioning. Mark was stumbling along, which caused the coach to feel we were all loafing. I think the coach wanted to teach us about teamwork. "OK, everyone, line up here and we will run one-hundred-yard dashes until we give it our all, together." We ran about five or six then saw that Mark was throwing up, but this time it was blood. He said, over and over again, "I will not quit; I will not quit." It turned out that he had a congenital heart disease of some kind. He knew it. His parents knew it. But he was determined to find out what it was like to be an athlete. He wanted to be one of us. He did not care if he played in a game; he wanted to be a part of a team. Later, as a freshman in college, I learned that Mark died of that disease. Often, when I am tired, hurting, or just feeling sorry for myself, I think back to those days with Mark and say to myself, "If he can be so determined to live life to the fullest, I have no right to quit or give up." A lesson in real life learned the hard way.

There is a fascinating story found in Acts 27:21–44. It is the story of Paul being taken as a prisoner to Rome after he declared the right of his Roman citizenship to be heard in Rome. A violent storm attacked the ship, putting all aboard at risk. "They prayed for daylight" (Acts 27:29 NIV). Been there, haven't you? Waiting for the hope of a new day. The sailors, the rough, tough, brave men, were about to escape the ship on a lifeboat. Paul knew the rest would die if the sailors deserted their posts. Here is how the scripture records it: "Then Paul said to the centurion and the soldiers, 'Unless these men stay with the ship, you cannot be saved.' So the soldiers cut the ropes that held the lifeboat and let it fall away" (Acts 27:31–32 NIV). A lesson in real life learned the hard way.

We all face times when we just feel tired; maybe *exhausted* is a better word. When will this circumstance end? That is our cry. We know life is difficult at times. We have experienced it on a daily basis. So many things just do not come easy for us, especially when it comes to faith, trust, and dependence on God. We want to give in, give up, and just jump ship. Maybe it is time to cut loose the lifeboats. We need to be more resolute in our determination to trust God in the most difficult matters of life. The psalmist said, "For his anger lasts only a moment, but his favor lasts a lifetime; weeping may remain for a night, but rejoicing comes in the morning" (Psalm 30:5 NIV). Usually, we doubt because we want a quick fix to our problems. Trust God's timing, God's way will become obvious to you. When you feel the pain of running the race of life is too much, remember those who had a good excuse to quit but never did. Let them be your inspiration to run faster, farther, and with greater determination. Cut loose your escape plan and stay on board, for God brings us all to safety. Never quit trying!

> God, we all too often learn our lessons in life the hard way. We end up saying we should have, could have, wish we had. Give us this day our daily dose of humility to submit to your plan so we can fulfill your purpose, your way. Let us never quit when the lesson is still before us. Amen.

"A Frog on a Lilypad on a Lake of Pain"

That is what the commercial says. The legal broker, sitting in his car, driving along, and talking about legal services, gives this strange quote: "A frog on a lily pad on a lake of pain." Really? I am not sure I get it. I guess he is appealing to those who are in pain due to an accident. Just an interesting statement. It does stick in your brain, so I guess we could say it is a good commercial. The question I ask today is this: do you know pain? We all have stories, don't we? Times when we have experienced pain. Broken bones, falls, car accidents, hitting your head on an open cabinet door, and on I could go. Pain is a part of life. That is what I told my five-year-old grandson when he fell yesterday.

There is pain worse than physical pain. There is mental pain. There is emotional pain. There is spiritual pain. We use words like *anguish*, *suffering*, *torment*, *agony*, *distress*, *grief*, *affliction*, and *anxiety* to talk about the pain we feel when our emotional, mental, and spiritual pain crash into one major feeling of pain. David, a spiritual king of Israel, who was more human like us than a spiritual giant, said it best. "When I kept silent, my bones wasted away through my groaning all day long. For day and night your hand was heavy upon me; my strength was sapped as in the heat of summer. Then I acknowledged my sin to you and did not cover up my iniquity. I said, 'I will confess my transgressions to the Lord'—and you forgave the guilt of my sin'" (Psalm 32:3–5 NIV).

In trying to understand why our world is in such a crisis of addiction, I have found some interesting facts. When I am talking about addiction, please understand I am talking about addiction to pain medication, alcohol, and illegal drugs that we use to numb our pain. What I have discovered is most professionals who deal with addiction will inform you that addiction begins when someone is feeling pain: physical, emotional, mental, or spiritual pain. It is a method to cover up those feelings. Then over time, the medication, illegal drugs, or alcohol begins to take over and life gets out of control. Life may be out of control, but the pain is still there hidden under the numbness. If a person is to deal with their addiction, they must deal with the causes of the pain that started them down the path of addiction. Cause and effect. That is when we discover the need for help. Professional help.

It is always better to deal with your pain upfront rather than fall prey to the artificial means, which just mask the issues. I think Paul and his thorn in the flesh (most likely physical pain) was a perfect example. Whatever his pain was, he prayed but it did not go away, so for him, he saw it as a way to stay humble. He used it to make himself a better servant of God. (2 Corinthians 12:7–10 NIV). David talks about dealing with pain (emotional, mental, and spiritual pain) when he says, "Blessed is he whose transgressions are forgiven, whose sins are covered. Blessed is the man whose sin the Lord does not count against him and in whose spirit is no deceit" (Psalm 32:1–2 NIV). David, out of the depths of his despair and anguish, discovered the only solution was to cry out to God with honest pleas for forgiveness and relief (Psalm 30:1; Psalm 130:1 NIV). He could keep silent no more. In his screams of pain, he found a real reprieve from his pain. Confession was not only good for his soul, but it also enabled him to live pain free through God's forgiveness.

Do not live alone with your pain. Do not mask your pain. Find strength to live with it or to relieve it through your prayers and faith in God. If you have an addiction, seek help from professionals and learn to trust God.

Dear Lord Jesus, because you live, we can face tomorrow. We know this. Let us face it with open honest expressions of who we are and what we need, with the faithful acceptance of all we face. Amen.

William P. (Buddy) Nelson

Angry at God?

We had all been asked to move to a back room near the ICU at Montclair Hospital. Families are isolated in situations such as this for one of two reasons, maybe both. It is either for our privacy or to keep us from upsetting the other families waiting for their loved ones. It is awkward. For whatever reason, when death is near, the hospitals move you to a room that was once a one-bed ICU room where they crowd twenty people inside to wait. This night started when Wayne, my brother-in-law (friend), called about midnight and said my sister, Carol Lois, had a stroke and was being brought to Birmingham by ambulance. He asked if I could meet him there. Slowly, all the family began to gather through the early morning hours. Carol Lois was not going to make it. There was "the process" to cut off the respirator. Agonizing hours slowly went by, until the time came and we all said goodbye. Forty-nine years old. It is not fair. I hear my father say over and over again a parent is not supposed to bury their child. In that moment, I felt angry with God. Why had this been allowed to happen? Pain. Tears. Loneliness. Grief.

Most of us in similar situations feel the emotions of being angry with God because there are no answers. We cannot explain it away. There must be acceptance before the real work of healing has time to set in.

It is interesting to find in Holy Scriptures stories where individuals get angry with God in a different way. We can understand anger in times of grief and sorrow. But do you remember when someone got very angry with God for doing what God promised to do? The man was asked to accomplish something great and wonderful for God, and when he was successful, he was angry. Listen to what is said before I tell you who. The name is altered to protect the guilty. "But (Buddy) was greatly displeased and became angry. He prayed to the Lord, 'O Lord, is this not what I said when I was still at home? That is why I was so quick to run from you … I knew that you are a gracious and compassionate God, slow to anger and abounding in love, a God who relents from sending calamity. Now, O Lord, take away my life, for it is better for me to die than to live.' But the Lord replied, 'Have you any right to be angry?'" (Jonah 4:1–4 paraphrased).

Yes, I am talking about Jonah. It is Jonah 4:1–4. Jonah after his experience in the whale. Jonah after he did what God had called him to do. Jonah after, with God's help, he had succeeded in saving the Ninevites from destruction. Angry with God because God was so compassionate that he wanted to save even the enemies of the Jewish people. He wanted to save those who were living the farthest from a godly lifestyle. Jonah was so angry with God that he wanted to die.

Stop for a minute today and think with me. Can we become guilty of transferring our anger toward people and allow that dislike, hatred, and animosity to become a grieflike anger toward God himself, if God wants to save them? It happened to Jonah. It can happen to us. If this is true, we need to be cautious of the quicksand we are treading upon. Words of conscience resonate in our heads like "Go ye …" (Matthew 28:18); "Love as …" (John 13:34); "Forgive to be forgiven …" (Matthew 6:14); and on and on it goes. This is where the real world crashes into the righteousness we are called to pursue. I struggle with these concepts, because I know how frail my emotions are when it comes to disliking others who have hurt me or my loved ones. Yet this is where we are. God wants us to face a Jonah-like struggle yet come out with a better attitude in the end. The book of Jonah ends with God saying his great truth. "Should I not be concerned about that great city?" (Jonah 4:11 NIV).

God of grace and God of glory, we know you understand us when we are angry, yet we seek your consolation and comfort for our grief and anger. Help us to do better in trusting you. Amen.

Life, ChaRacteR, aNd YouR SouL

I n 1 Kings 21, we discover the story of King Ahab, Queen Jezebel, and Naboth. It is a story of greed, trickery, deception, and murder. It would be a perfect story line for Crime Stoppers. Naboth had a vineyard. Ahab wanted it. He wanted it so badly that Jezebel plotted through lies and deception to have Naboth killed so Ahab could take position of the vineyard. It is interesting that together Ahab and Jezebel break four of the Ten Commandments: murder, steal, false witness, and covet (Exodus 20:1–21). I guess this would put them in the category of Bonnie and Clyde.

A few questions come to mind. First, what is a man's life worth? Second, what is your character worth? Finally, what value do you put on your soul? The value of a person's life, the quality of a person's character, and our willingness to sell our soul on the altar of whatever comes our way seem to be the big issues of our day. These are issues that have been in our world since Adam and Eve and Cain and Able. Issues that will always be with us as long as we are on this earth. They are issues that test our beliefs and our faithfulness. I must admit I often fail the test. It is not enough to simply confess our weaknesses. We need to figure out a better approach in life.

What is a person's life worth? When we hear stories of people held captive as prisoners of war, we believe the value of human life was not much to the captors. When others listen to how we talk about people we do not like, they might believe we do not value human life. When we hear modern-day stories of greed, there seems to be no value to human life at all unless it is your own. A better approach in life might be to always try to see value in another person, even if they have wronged you. Jesus would say, "Love as I have loved you" (John 13:34 NIV). If he loves us, there is something in us worth loving. If he loves others, we must strive to find something in them worth loving.

What is your character worth? Your character is your reputation. It is what people see in you that makes you special. You can hide your true self with a smile, but your character comes out in the way you live every day. My father had a deep-seated weakness when he saw one particular character flaw in other people. If a person lied to him, he found it very difficult to forgive them. It was, in part, the unpardonable sin to my dad. He once said if a person lies to you, it says volumes as to what kind of a person they are. You just cannot trust them. That was his lesson to me when he caught me lying. The truth and nothing but the truth, right? Son, the most valuable aspect of your life is your character. Protect it with your life. A better approach might be, to be truth tellers. Jesus said, "Let your yes be yes and your no, no" (Matthew 5:37 NIV).

On what altar will you sell your soul? The god of Baal, like Jezebel wanted Ahab to sell out for? No. But we often sell our soul for covetous needs, for political beliefs, for indwelling hatred, for anything we desire when we believe we are right. Can you believe it? We are not always right! Sometimes we are blinded by the things we want and fail to see a better idea or way of life. A better approach might be to learn to listen to all sides, gather all facts, and make personal choices based on facts, not on manipulations. Ahab would have been better off if he had not listened to Jezebel, right?

> God, we know you understand us and our weaknesses. You understand us even when our ambitions get in the way. May our lives not become a distraction which causes others to fail to know Christ. Forgive us, this day, for not listening to you more. Assist us in finding your way of love. Help us to value life, develop faithful character, and commit our souls to you and you alone. Amen.

Where Are You?

It was a beautiful day. Several friends and I had gone into the woods across the street on the back side of our house. It was my favorite place to play. There were rocks to climb. A creek to play in and catch crawfish. Vines to swing on. A perfect place for ten-year-old kids to play. One problem: Mother said, "Do not go into those woods to play." The bell rang, calling me to supper, then came that loud voice, which still echoes in my ears so many years later, "Buddy, where are you?" I could not believe it. The perfect playtime disrupted by the call to supper. I had a plan, however. I ran to the end of the wooded area following the creek, came out of the woods at the end of the street, then came walking down the street as if I had been over to a friend's house. Mother said to wash up for supper. My immediate thoughts were of victory! I got away with it! Washed up, came to supper, bowed for our prayer with a smirk on my face, and the meal began. Then suddenly it began! The itch on my legs, then my hands, then my neck, then all over. I could not stand it. Mother ask what the matter was, and I said I was itching all over. Literally all over. I had the worst case of poison ivy the world had ever seen. The lotion, the Benadryl, and then, "Where were you?" The confession came. "I was in the woods." I have now made my point for this devotion, so I will not go further in what happened after that moment in time.

Where are you? Are you where God wants you to be? Are you doing what God wants you to do? Are you being the kind of person God wants you to be? These are questions that could break the heart of God if they point out we are walking the path set out before us or if we are going off on our own path. We all too often make poor choices.

"Then the man and his wife heard the sound of the Lord God as he was walking in the garden in the cool of the day, and they hid from the Lord God among the trees of the garden. But the Lord God called to the man, 'Where are you?' He answered, 'I heard you in the garden, and I was afraid because I was naked; so, I hid'" (Genesis 3:8–10 NIV). This is the recording of the first faith crisis in the history of humankind. The resulting guilt of sin. Where are you? The confrontation between a loving God, who gave us everything, and the first two humans choosing to partake of the only thing that God said to leave alone. When a person sins, they want to hide. Hide from parents, hide from the law, hide from society, hide from friends, hide from God.

Where are you? Today, as you are preparing for your day, or if you are finishing your day, ask yourself this question: "Where am I?" God wants us to choose to be obedient, faithful, loving, kind, compassionate, and spiritually fit for the battle of life. There are so many things that can get us off the path where God is leading us. Do not become distracted by those who tempt us. Do not be distracted by those who want to manipulate us. Do not be distracted by greener pastures. Do not be distracted by the woods across the street from your home. Follow the teachings of God and not the half truths of other people. Decide for yourself! I choose to be where God wants me to be! What say you?

God of truth and perfection, guide our lives as we move together with the purity of your good news into the chaos of this world. Let us be found where you choose for us to be, doing what you choose for us to be doing. May we overcome the chaos rather than being overcome by it. Amen.

Escape Plan

I
n their 1965 album, the Animals sang, "We gotta get out of this place, if it's the last thing we ever do."[7] In one sense, it was a tragic way of looking at life. In another way, it has become the cry of so many people whenever we are overwhelmed with the problems in our society that seem unresolvable. Let's just get out of here. Let's develop an escape plan. Run, even if you do not know where you are going.

A religious manifestation of this escape plan mentality seems to be praying for Christ to return *now*. There is a passage in Luke 21:5–36 where Jesus is responding to his disciples' question "When will these things happen?" (Luke 21:7 NIV). Beginning from that moment in time until this very day, people are asking, "When, Lord?" Many people have spent a lifetime developing charts, writing books, and preaching that the time is near. It seems that many people want it to happen right now, so we do not have to deal with all of the issues we face in our society. To me it is an ostrich approach whereby we put our heads in the sand and hope it all goes away.

What does Jesus say?

He gives a great description of the kinds of things that will happen in Luke 21:8–36. In his way, he is telling us it will happen. We are to anticipate it. We are to believe it. We are to look for his coming. However, Jesus also says, "No one knows about that day or hour, not even the angels in heaven, nor the Son, but only the Father. Be on guard! Be alert! You do not know when that time will come" (Mark 13:32–33 NIV). He also says, "Therefore go and make disciples of all nations, baptizing them in

---

[7] The Animals, "We Gotta Get Out Of This Place," 1965. Copyright by EMI Publishing.

the name of the Father and of the Son and of the Holy Spirit, and teaching them to obey everything I have commanded you. And surely, I am with you always, to the very end of the age" (Matthew 28:19–20 NIV).

Why am I rambling about this today? Focus! We do not need to cry, "We gotta get out of this place …" We do not need to think, *Hurry up, God.* We do not need an escape plan. God has already provided one for us. If we believe God sent his Son, Jesus, into the world because he loved us, that he died and suffered for our sins, was buried, and rose on the third day, and that he is coming again, we are saved. If we die, we will be with him in heaven. If he returns before then, we will be gathered with the saints. Our future is assured. What shall we do with the life we have here on earth until that time?

Jesus says, "As long as it is day, we must do the work of him who sent me. Night is coming, when no one can work" (John 9:4 NIV). Notice the "we" must work and the "who sent me." This interplay of words is significant. Christ was sent to put us to work! For further study, read 1 Thessalonians 4 and 5. You will note how much is about living daily the life Christ wants us to live. "Make it your ambition to lead a quiet life, to mind your own business and to work with your hands, just as we told you" (1 Thessalonians 4:11 NIV). The rest is assuring us of his return. "For the Lord himself will come down from heaven, with a loud command, with the voice of the archangel and with the trumpet call of God, and the dead in Christ will rise first. After that, we who are still alive and are left will be caught up together with them in the clouds to meet the Lord in the air. And so we will be with the Lord forever. Therefore encourage each other with these words" (1 Thessalonians 4:16–18 NIV). Beautiful contrast. "Do the work and be encouraged." Do you remember the old hymn written by Anna L. Coghill with the lyrics "Work, for the night is coming, when man's work is done"? There is a story to tell; there is a job to be done. We are placed here in this world at a time like this because God needs us to carry out his mission. The darker the night that overcomes the world, the brighter the hope that we find in Jesus. Let's get to work rather than looking for an escape plan. God needs us to be his people, doing his work, his way, in a world lost in the darkness of sin. Will we be his light of hope, or will we choose to run away from the responsibility he has entrusted us with to change the world?

I pray, Father, that you will find us faithful in the challenge to be in this world at this time to bring about hope, peace, joy, and love in a world that does not know any of it. Bring a renewal of your people so the lost world will be reached. May we no longer look for an escape plan but be about your kingdom work. Amen.

Who Is First?

n 1937, Bud Abbott and Lou Costello first did their hilarious routine "Who's on First?" It is still a classic today. If you have not seen it, or if you want to see it again, just search YouTube for "Who's on First video." It will brighten your day. It contrasts a play on words and names related to baseball. Yesterday, however, I felt as if I were amid a "Who *is* first" routine, which was humorous yet very dangerous. It seemed to be a competition as to who was the first in line. I was driving down Interstate 20 toward Birmingham. I was driving seventy-two miles per hour. (Someone once told me the state troopers set their radar at seventy-five miles per hour.) Then zoom! Cars, eighteen-wheelers, and other vehicles began to fly past me. I could not even estimate the speed. My first subconscious reaction was to begin slowly to speed up. Suddenly, I was close to seventy-eight miles per hour. Then one car came weaving from one lane to the next, cutting so close that I slowed down, expecting a wreck. Suddenly, another car, which had been cut off a bit, zoomed out, and the race was on. They seemed to be trying to prove who was first!

We live in a very competitive society. We believe in winners. We all want to be number 1. We want to be first. First Americans in space on a privately owned rocket. The race to be first with a COVID-19 vaccine. First in sports. First in state championships. First to get to the lunch table at school. First in class grades. First to memorize the books of the Bible. First to come back to church. First in line at a concert. First to climb Mount Everest. First to discover America. First to win a marathon. And on the list can go and does go continuously every day. Who is first?

Becky and I had fun the rest of the day making comments and saying,

"I'm first. Turn here. I was planning to do that. But I'm first." You know how conversations can go. Who is *first?*

It began to dawn on me that maybe this was the reason we have so much trouble understanding and living by the teachings of Jesus. His teachings run so contrary to human nature and especially the American way of life. Jesus said, "They came to Capernaum. When he was in the house, he asked them, 'What were you arguing about on the road?' But they kept quiet because on the way they had argued about who was the greatest. Sitting down, Jesus called the Twelve and said, 'If anyone wants to be first, he must be the very last, and the servant of all'" (Mark 9:33–36 NIV). Jesus had said earlier, "'If anyone would come after me, he must deny himself and take up his cross and follow me'" (Mark 8:34 NIV).

It is one thing to believe Jesus was real. That is head knowledge. That is using reason and facts. When a person determines to live the life of a Christ follower, that is something entirely different. That is heart knowledge. This is when all of our emotions and senses come together recognizing what God has done for us in Jesus. This necessary step takes us out of the competitive nature of life and creates within us a heavenly desire to utilize our lives to serve and help others. It is the "Love as I have loved you" (John 13:34 NIV) philosophy, which is the CHANGE aspect of following Christ. Who is first? It should be Jesus and his kingdom (Matthew 6:33 NIV).

> God of grace and God of mercy, give us a change in attitude so we are not desiring worldly things. May our heart's desire be to serve and follow you. May we believe with our heads and our hearts. May we slow down and find new joy in not trying to be first. Amen.

Understanding versus Confusion: Reading Scripture

Multiple issues arise in which it is difficult to comprehend what is meant for confusion and what is meant for understanding. This is especially true when it comes to reading, understanding, and sometimes becoming confused by scripture. For some people, this comes across as frustration. I have a different way of addressing it. I see it as God's way of making us work for our understanding rather than spoon feeding us. In addition, I am amazed that in different circumstances the Bible beautifully and clearly speaks its truth in different ways. Let me try to help you understand what I am talking about while trying to avoid confusion.

I wrote a devotion titled "Who Is First?" In the words I penned, I mentioned the difference between head knowledge and heart knowledge. Read again to what I said. "It is one thing to believe Jesus was real. That is head knowledge. That is using reason and facts. When a person determines to live the life of a Christ follower, that is something entirely different. That is heart knowledge. This is when all of our emotions and senses come together recognizing what God has done for us in Jesus."

This triggered within my soul a thought that has been impossible to shake loose. I wonder if this may be what the book of Acts is referencing in Acts 8:14–17. This passage is dealing with the spread of the Gospel and some of the challenges faced by the newest converts. There is a lot of interplay and confusion. "When the apostles in Jerusalem heard that Samaria had accepted the word of God, they sent Peter and John to them. When they arrived, they prayed for them that they might receive the Holy Spirit, because the Holy Spirit had not yet come upon any of them; they had simply been baptized into the name of the Lord Jesus. Then Peter and John placed their hands on them, and they received the Holy Spirit" (Acts 8:14–17 NIV).

Depending on your previous experiences and teachings while growing up, there are different thoughts in scripture about the Holy Spirit. Some see it as a purely special gift of healing or speaking in a heavenly language. Paul talks about speaking in unknown tongues (1 Corinthians 14:17–18 NIV) himself. He does say it can be confusing and gives guidance as to how to address it in the church (1 Corinthians 14:1–33 NIV). The day of Pentecost was different. When God moved amid the disciples, they spoke, and all who heard, heard in their own language. Yet here in Acts 8 and in other passages, there seems to be another way to understand the reference to the Holy Spirit. What clicked in my thoughts was this: what if this reference to "accepting the word of God … yet the Holy Spirit had not come upon them" (Acts 8:15–16 NIV) means these people had a head knowledge of Jesus but had not developed a heart knowledge of him? Maybe they had not developed the heart knowledge that changes us, so all of our emotions and senses come together recognizing what God has done for us in Jesus. Personally, I think some may speak in unknown tongues today as their personal experience. I do not myself. Yet I do believe a follower of Christ, a true follower of Christ, must move from being a church attender to becoming an "all-in ambassador for Christ"— taking head knowledge and transforming it into heart knowledge. "Do not conform any longer to the pattern of this world but be transformed by the renewing of your mind. Then you will be able to test and approve what God's will is—his good, pleasing and perfect will" (Romans 12:2 NIV). Are we transformed Christians living a life of heartfelt emotions and giving our all for Christ?

Heavenly Father, motivate us beyond being church members. May we be transformed into heart-knowledge servants for you with clarity of purpose and understanding. Amen.

Do You Want to See God?

The decision to go into ministry is an easy one for many people who are called into ministry. This was not my personal experience. As Becky sometimes says, "You overanalyze things." This is a very true statement. My mind works in a way where I am seeking the logical, rational, and provable results of questions and ideas. When I was feeling called, I tried to utilize these methods so I could give a logical answer rather than an emotional solution. Cognitive reason. That's the phrase! I finally sat back and literally said, "OK, God, if you appear to me like you did Paul on the road to Damascus, I will do whatever you ask." Wait for it. Wait for it. Nothing happened. Then reading further in scripture, I came across passages like "O you of little faith!" (Matthew 6:30 NIV) and "Where is your faith?" (Luke 8:25 NIV). The revelation that was mine that day was it is faith that draws us into the presence of God. Then when in the presence of God, some interesting things begin to happen. Paul's experience was a unique experience for him and why God needed him. I recognized my calling was to be different from Paul's even though the same God was calling me for his plan he had for me.

Look at Exodus 3:1–6. This is Moses's experience of the burning bush and his encounter with the living God. It was his story of calling in a tremendous moment in time where there needed to be a mighty movement for God that would reach out to his people in need of a Savior. In this mountaintop experience, I want us to consider five words that seem to describe what happened in the soul of Moses when he felt the presence of a mighty God.

The first is amazement. Moses was filled with wonder, shock, and astonishment. He could not believe something was happening and he was a witness to that event. It drew him into God's holy place. The second is curiosity. Being drawn into the holy place of God, he wanted to know more, understand more, and experience more. It is like a person being amazed by something about a church and being drawn into that church to see for themselves and wanting to know more. The third is worship. Once in the holy place, he heard the voice of God and fell, like the wise men at Jesus's birth, and worshiped. It was not because it was Sunday and a service was planned; it was a spontaneous worship that came from his heart. That's worship, isn't it? The fourth is fear. Moses's fear was because he knew God was there and because he knew God was calling him and because he feared failing God. The final one is focus. All this experience brought Moses's life into focus. It guided his every step from that moment forward. His life was to fulfill God's calling to lead God's people.

Christ followers need to have a Moses type of calling today! I believe in the depths of my soul that God is calling a church, in a tremendous moment in time, where there needs to be a mighty movement for God that will reach out to his people in need of the Savior. A church that will say, "Here we are, Lord; use us" (Genesis 22:4; Exodus 3:4; Joshua 14:10; and 1 Samuel 3:1–10 NIV). A church that will open its doors and hearts to offer this world the hope that is available only through Jesus. A church that will rise above strife and the issues of the day and bring back the Holy purpose of God's plan for the church. Will we be that church? If we come into his presence to see him, we will become that church, changed forever! Do you want to see God?

Amazing God, the one who creates within us a curiosity that leads us to worship you, the God who brings to us sufficient fear to enable us to focus on the task before us, allow us the privilege of becoming the beginning of a mighty movement in this tremendous moment of time. May your kingdom on earth be rediscovered and we as your people be faithful to you and you alone. Amen.

How Do You Win an Argument?

Growing up was not an easy process, and I know it is not yet complete. When I go through the files in my mind of the different stages of growing up, I see that a lot had to do with how I was able, or not able, to handle disagreements and bullying. I really did not handle them well. Sometimes I feel that I revert to my old ways, and it causes me to stop and think, *Do not go there, Buddy.* Early on, and I know people who have known me will not believe it, I felt bullied. I was slow, fat, and very clumsy. Mother called me awkward. Daddy, in frustration, said once, "You will never amount to anything." Kids at school seemed to see me as fresh meat and picked on me, mainly because I would not fight back. One day before school, as we were waiting on the doors to open, a guy said something and I exploded. I balled up my fist, took a swing, and busted him right in the mouth. His mouth was bleeding, my knuckle was bleeding, but I walked away two feet taller. *No one will bother me now!* That was when a coach discovered a potential recruit. I confess my struggle with anger continued for many years.

During the years to come, I recognized that you do not need to win arguments and disagreements by being more aggressive than the opponent. You can actually have disagreements, arguments, and even heated discussions and still walk away friends. Today, some of my closest friends are people I disagree with, but we have decided to be friends first and have healthy conversations anyway. Why do we today feel we have to always win by putting the other person down? Why can we not have healthy dialogue? Why can we not sit down and agree to disagree at times? This attitude of having to win the argument, no matter the cost, is what is hurting our Christian witness. It is hurting and dividing churches. It is making our American political system totally dysfunctional. We are leaving no room for forgiveness or compromise.

How do you win an argument? Let me remind you that no matter what the issue might be, we must, at all times and in all ways, never stray away from our Christian principles. Spreading rumors, hate talk, conspiracy theories, and believing anything the TV or the internet says is not the way of Christ. Look with me to Colossians 3:12–17. If you want to win an argument by balling up your fist and taking a swing at another person physically or verbally, remember that is inconsistent with these words: "Clothe yourselves with compassion, kindness, humility, gentleness and patience. Bear with one another and forgive whatever grievances you might have against one another" (Colossians 3:12–13 NIV).

I choose to dedicate my life, my energy, and my efforts, as imperfect as I am, toward empowering people to stand firm in their faith without bringing disrespect on the truth of Christ's message. I choose to empower people in finding ways to sit down and talk about differences so there can be a consensus of what is best for all people. I choose to remain an Alabama fan while respecting those who choose to be Auburn fans. I choose to be diligent in making recommendations to the church I serve, reserving the right to be outvoted. I choose to proclaim God's Word without comingling it in politics. I choose to listen more than I self-declare. I choose to be an example of Christ rather than feeling I have to win every argument by destroying another person.

God of peace, love, and truth, empower us to put down our weapons of strife in our country and learn to sit down and talk. Help us to get to know each other better, feel each other's pain, and above all else seek ways to show Christ through our words, actions, motives, and attitudes. Let us not be like Cain, the Pharisees, or Judas. Let us learn to be like Christ. Amen.

Being Tested

My favorite part of the educational process was the surprise we received when the teacher walked into the room and said, "Put everything away except your pencil. We are having a pop test today to see what you have learned." I was kidding when I said that was my favorite part of education. It increased my heart rate, my hands became sweaty, and usually my brain froze. Tests, sudden or planned, were never fun. Tests were always feared because the results determined your grades. The grades determined how pleased the parents were and whether you could go on to the next grade. Any slipup and you could be in trouble. How did you like being tested?

Athletes are tested every day at practices and in games. It is a time of perfecting skill, strength, and success. The end result was to determine how much improvement you made daily, weekly, and in a game. If you were unable to pass the test, then the next person up would win your position. If you were an athlete, how did you like being tested?

Every day we are being tested as faith believers. Every day is an opportunity for us to see what we have learned. Every day is an opportunity to prove we are improving and growing in our spiritual strength and knowledge. Every situation we face, good or bad, is going to prove in a tangible way who we are and what we believe. As a Christ follower, how do you like being tested?

In Matthew 4, we find Jesus's temptations. The Greek word for *tempted* is *peirazo*. This word is translated as *examination, examine, try, prove,* or *tempted.* If Jesus is God wrapped in human flesh, then why was he tempted or tested in the wilderness? You know there is a plan or purpose for everything Christ did. In my thoughts, Jesus was tested and proved faithful, so when we are tested, we will know that God understands what it is to be tested. He is a compassionate God who wants us to know he loves and understands. Every day, he does this while testing/tempting our faithfulness.

We find these curious words in John when Jesus was answering the question presented by the disciples: "'Neither this man nor his parents sinned,' said Jesus, 'but this happened so that the work of God might be displayed in his life'" (John 9:3 NIV). This comes from the story of the man born blind. The disciples were asking, in their old way of thinking, "Did his mother or father cause this by their sin? (John 9:2 NIV)." Jesus said, "Neither." It is not the way you have thought about things in the past. You need to think about it in new terms. This has happened so "the work of God might be displayed in his life." This was another test for the disciples to think in new terms, not in old terms. Paul says, "To be made new in the attitude of your minds; and to put on the new self, created to be like God in true righteousness and holiness" (Ephesians 4:23–24 NIV). That's our daily test, is it not? We must answer every attitude we have with every old idea that comes our way and interpret life with the new attitude we find in Christ. How do you like being tested?

Maybe we need to ask questions like, as a person who wants to follow the teachings of Christ, the following:

- How do we look at life in crisis, whether it is a pandemic or any crisis that comes our way?
- How do we look at the political divide in our nation?
- How do we look at racism in the world?
- How do we look at our own personal problems?
- How do you like being tested?

God, who humbles us every day, help us to keep our hearts open, our knees bent, and our eyes open for what you want from each of us. Let us be found faithful in every test in life. Amen.

Memories

Cleaning out another box in my basement, I came across some things that were amazing to me. One item was the book *I Will Follow Jesus* by Elizabeth Norton Jones. This book was the guide used by Herbert Sargent of First Baptist Church of Greenville, South Carolina, to assist me in understanding the decision I had made to become a Christian, when I was nine years old. Another item discovered was the obituary card from the first funeral I ever performed. It was in Leitchfield, Kentucky, on April 13, 1976. The lady who had passed, Sally Green, was the mother of Edith Gaither, a member of the church I pastored while in seminary. The payment I received for that service was a hand-sewn teddy bear that she made for our son Bill. I think he still has it. Another item discovered was a copy of the first sermon I ever preached: "My First Sermon: Text: 2 Corinthians 5:17, June 24, 1973." This was twenty-three days after Becky and I were married. I will confess it was not a very good sermon, but it was my first opportunity to share what God had been doing in my life. Memories.

This triggered within my soul the following question: "What are the things we remember about life, people, and places?" As we are getting older, we may not remember why we stood up to do something, but we usually have memories of past years. What do you remember? What has influenced your life? Who had the greatest impact on your life? If I asked you to immediately respond to the question "Where was your favorite place to go," what would you say? Memories.

Now a shift in our thought processes. How do you want people to remember you and the things you did in this life? You may want to write them down so a preacher one day will have a better idea how to talk about your life. Your memories.

In 1 Peter 5 are some interesting thoughts given to elders and young people. I encourage you to read the entire chapter. Look closely at some words used: "humble, cast off anxiety, self-controlled, alert, stand firm" (1 Peter 5:6–9 NIV). Would it not be a great testimony to a life well lived for people who knew you to be able to say you were humble not arrogant, calm not anxious, under control not out of control, alert to what was happening so you were not manipulated, and you always stood firm in faith rather than running in fear? Memories made by your life experiences, not made up about your life.

This chapter, 1 Peter 5, ends in an interesting way. The words resonate with hope and a reason to live that kind of life. In 1 Peter 5:10–11 (NIV), we read about God's grace, how we are to keep our eyes on the eternal, and yes, we will suffer in this life, but God makes us strong, firm, and steadfast. In other words, his grace refreshes us with the daily renewed ability to live our life where memories are remarkably worth remembering. A life well lived because we lived the way God intended us to live. Read verses 6–9 again. "Humble yourselves, therefore, under God's mighty hand, that he may lift you up in due time. Cast all your anxiety on him because he cares for you. Be self-controlled and alert. Your enemy the devil prowls around like a roaring lion looking for someone to devour. Resist him, standing firm in the faith, because you know that your brothers throughout the world are undergoing the same kind of sufferings" (1 Peter 5:6–9 NIV).

"Humble, cast off anxiety, self-controlled, alert, stand firm" (1 Peter 5:6–9 NIV). That is it! Memories made while we live our lives for Christ. Not only are they memories worth remembering, but we also become his example to others. Have you figured it out yet? We as Christ followers face the same difficult issues as do those who have no faith. We, however, see our challenges as opportunities to be witnesses. Because of God's grace, we can be different, unique, and worth remembering. Memories.

God who changed us, give us this day our measure of renewed ability to face the challenges of life and live a life worth remembering. May the way we live help another person to know the value of believing in Christ. Amen.

Can There Be a Conversation?

D o you remember the old question "When a tree falls in a forest, when no one is around, does it make a sound?" (This phrase appears to have originated in the 1910 book *Physics* by Charles Riborg Mann and George Ransom Twiss.) The answer is yes. Sound waves are generated by the reverberations of breaking roots and branches and the crash of the tree to the ground. The problem is that the sound waves finally fade out before anyone is available to hear.

Conversation is a two-way street. There must be a speaker and a listener. Healthy conversation is a bit different. Healthy conversation takes place when both individuals decide to speak and to listen. It truly involves four of our five senses. In healthy conversation, we need to use our mouths, our ears, our sight, and our sense of touch or feeling. Speak your truth with a willingness to hear the other person's concerns and see the emotions in their face and body language. Then hold out your hand as proof you both have come to some understanding. You can disagree without being angry. That, to me, is healthy conversation. Christians need more healthy conversations. Our nation needs more healthy conversations. Understanding racial divides need more healthy conversations. Marriages need more healthy conversations. We all need to learn how to have more healthy conversations.

In 2 Corinthians 5:16–21, we find an interesting section of Paul's letter to Corinth. He is making a powerful statement of how the church is to look at worldly events yet remain godly. Look at the following three verses with me:

1. "So from now on we regard no one from a worldly point of view" (2 Corinthians 5:16 NIV).

2. "If anyone is in Christ, they are a new creation" (2 Corinthians 5:17 NIV).
3. "We are therefore Christ's ambassadors, as though God were making his appeal through us" (2 Corinthians 5:20 NIV).

Where do we find healthy Christian conversation today? Why is it we feel if someone disagrees with us we have to categorize them as the enemy? Where have all the civil dialogues gone in the world today? How in God's name are we to have a positive effect on our world today, which desperately needs it, unless we are willing to have healthy conversations?

My appeal to you today, which is also an appeal for my own self-awareness, is that as faith followers we learn to speak as if God were speaking through us. Take the time to understand the other person. Ask questions. Why do you feel that way? What has your experience been in the past? What has caused your hurt? How can I assist you? How can I get involved? Then and only then, express in love how you feel.

If we are to be Christ's ambassadors, it is more important to listen and share love than it is to simply state your argument as to why you are right. You might not be. We need to learn how to talk about faith. We need to learn how to talk about politics. We should learn how to talk about race. We should learn how to talk about a world in crisis. Yes, we should learn how to talk about all the issues in a healthy, healing way! Be Christ's ambassadors! Do not be dividers! Is this not what Christ asks of us?

Gracious Heavenly Father, teach us your language of truth with love. Help us to overcome our prejudices, our hate, and our inflexible attitudes so we can make a positive impact on our world as your ambassadors. Amen.

Do-Overs: Don't You Wish

When someone says my freshman year in college was not my best and brightest days, they are being generous. Let me just express it in academic terms. I spent the next four and a half years making up for the first semester. If you wish, you can translate that into any other aspect of my life during that semester. One of my freshman classes was Western civilization, which was taught by Mrs. Mary Washington. I knew her because I had gone out with her daughter once in high school. I thought this would be a breeze with Mrs. Washington. The day came for the first exam. When I received my test paper after being graded, I was in shock. She had given me the grade of twenty-six. Yes, that's twenty-six out of one hundred. After class I went to her and said, "I know I did not do as well as I could have, but I did not do this bad, did I?" She did not answer the question. She never answered the question. She simply said, "I will make a deal with you. If you will average at least a B+ on the rest of the exams, and not miss another class, and not even be late to one of my classes, I will throw this test out. However, if you do not do what I have asked, I will average this test in with the rest." That was one of the few do-overs I was ever given. And yes, I took advantage of it!

In Acts 9, Dr. Luke recorded the most extensive account of Saul's conversion. Verses 4–6 are most vital to understand what was happening in the heart and mind of the man who would soon be called Paul. "He fell to the ground and heard a voice say to him, 'Saul, Saul, why do you persecute me?' 'Who are you, Lord?' Saul asked. 'I am Jesus, whom you are persecuting,' he replied. 'Now get up and go into the city, and you will be told what you must do'" (Acts 9:4–6 NIV). A real encounter with the presence of Christ. The miracle of light and a voice from heaven.

A confrontation of the horrific problem Paul was creating. Paul was persecuting Christ and his church. But where is the "because of your sin, you are going to hell"? Instead, there is this compassionate appeal as if the words are saying your sin is obvious but you are needed in this new message from God. This is the message all those who are lost in sin need to hear. The encouraging message of compassion and need. In other words, no matter what you have been doing, I still love you. In short, Saul had a do-over! As we have come to recognize, he took advantage of the opportunity and helped guide the church he once persecuted to be the church Christ intended it to be.

Allow me to ask a question. What has our evangelistic witnessing become today? Compassion or judgment? Maybe I have had too much time at home during this pandemic and it is making me too philosophical. Just follow my thoughts. Yes, a person who is living without faith in Christ is lost.

"Jesus answered, 'I am the way and the truth and the life. No one comes to the Father except through me'" (John 14:6 NIV). Yes, it is necessary to confess our sins to find forgiveness.

"That if you confess with your mouth, 'Jesus is Lord,' and believe in your heart that God raised him from the dead, you will be saved" (Romans 10:9 NIV).

Yes, we have a compassionate desire to encourage our friends and loved ones to find what we have found. Whatever happened to our desire to reach out into the world with the truth of Jesus's love even though we are sinners? Maybe it is time to offer those we know who are lost a do-over. "I know where you stand in relationship to Christ, yet I want you to know he still loves you and needs you, and so do I." I just ask you to process this idea and pray about it. A do-over changed my life. A do-over changed the life of Saul. What might a do-over do for those without Christ?

> God of the second chance, the third chance, and God of love and forgiveness, allow us to find our voice as Christ followers so we can, with your help, change the world. Amen.

My Prayer

"For this reason I remind you to fan into flame the gift of God, which is in you through the laying on of my hands" (2 Timothy 1:6 NIV). "Pray continually" (1 Thessalonians 5:17 NIV).

Sitting down each morning to write these devotionals has become a wonderful motivation for me. It helps prevent me from becoming complacent. It is so easy to fall into the trap of lethargy, laziness, and lack of purpose. My day begins with thoughts of *What shall I say today?* I do hope some of the words I share are beneficial to some of you. The real purpose of writing is for me to be doing something useful in an attempt to stay connected to others in need of encouragement as best I can under the circumstances. In reality, it is my daily reminder "to fan the flames of God's gift of salvation" (2 Timothy 1:6 NIV). I swell up with the desire to pray continually for us all. So today I want to share with you my prayer for today.

I pray that what we have discovered during this crisis will be a new beginning of how we as a family of faith can connect with the community in ways we have never thought of before. This will take an investment of time, energy, finances, and determination. We must constantly search for new ways of doing God's work. If we do not, we will become ineffective.

I pray that we will remember the past without becoming entrenched there. There are lessons to be learned. There are examples to follow. There is a heritage of how we became who we are today. There is also the need to understand today, which leads us into the future. We must be an effective family of faith ministering to families with children, young people, as well as senior adults. The church family that is satisfied is the church family that has no vision.

I pray that we will not walk backward into God's plan. We need to set goals, dream dreams, and see visions of what we can become with God's guidance. Can we ever truly be satisfied if we are not where God wants us to be, doing what God wants us to do, and being a loud voice in our community for what is right in God's eyes? We need to cast off every weight and run the race of life as Paul instructs us.

I pray that we will constantly believe God is in control—being prayer warriors rather than complainers; being spiritual visionaries rather than situational reactionaries; being meat seekers of the Gospel rather than being satisfied with only the milk of the Gospel (1 Corinthians 3:2 NIV).

I pray that we will love each other and love others as we know Christ has loved us (John 13:34 NIV). Faith with no action is not faith (James 2:18–19 NIV). If we believe, we are compelled to respond to that belief through our changed life. How can we ever be the same? When we are cleansed from our sin, like the leper we must run back to Jesus in appreciation (Luke 17:11–19 NIV). That is when we start understanding the "unto the least of these" (Matthew 25:40 and 45 KJV) challenges Jesus gave.

I pray that we will be a family of faith built on the foundation of God's Holy Word with the absolute belief in the reality of Jesus Christ. A church family that believes in discipling each other, reaching out to others, and knowing we are a part of God's plan for his kingdom on earth, filled with prayer warriors and doers of the faith. A church unified for the challenges we shall face in the days ahead.

Heavenly Father, may it be so! Amen.

A Simple Event in a Tumultuous Year

The Dow was at 850. A new house averaged $32,500. Gas was forty cents per gallon. The Vietnam War ended. Secretariat won the Triple Crown. Roe v. Wade was heard before the US Supreme Court. The World Trade Centers were completed. The Watergate trial began. Skylab was launched. It was a tumultuous year to say the least. Could anything good come out of such a year? Well, at 7 p.m. at the First Baptist Church of Beaumont, Texas, Becky and I said, "I do," and we began our lives together as husband and wife. It was one of the best years I have ever had. Forty-seven years later, our love is stronger than we ever thought it could be. With the birth of children, facing challenges, adjusting to the idea of "us" rather than "me," God has blessed each step of our path. I am blessed God allowed our life journeys to cross and we began to walk together down God's planned path.

I cannot help but smile whenever I read Ephesians 5:22–33. Paul takes three verses to inform a wife of her responsibilities. He then takes nine verses to tell the husband of his responsibilities. I guess, being a man, he knew how much more it took to get through the stubborn minds of men than it did women. I am an example of that stubbornness. There are three catchphrases that seem to make a clear statement, while the rest of the verses are definitions. One is "Wives, submit to your husbands as to the Lord" (Ephesians 5:22 NIV). Most men would prefer to leave it at that. Another is "Husbands, love your wives, just as Christ loved the church and gave himself up for her" (Ephesians 5:25 NIV). These two, however, can easily be falsely interpreted if we do not include the third phrase found in verse 21. This is the verse that is too often left out in our understanding of a Christian marriage. It is the ribbon that ties all the proper understanding together into a healthy relationship. It reads, "Submit to one another out of reverence to Christ" (Ephesians 5:21 NIV). The idea of a wife submitting and a husband loving like Christ are ways of defining how we are to submit to each other. It is not one or the other; it is both. Loving like Christ is submitting, isn't it? Christian marriage is a partnership. Two believers sharing life together submitting to one another out of a love that is so unique that it is like the love Christ has for his church.

Does that mean our marriage has been perfect? Does that mean we have never had arguments? Does that mean we have been perfect through these forty-eight years? No. No. No. This means we have had this biblical ideal before us, and we have striven to reach that goal. We are not there yet, but it is what keeps us together, even during the toughest years. We have realized how important it is to translate the word *submit* into the idea of *koinonia* (Christian love). That is the giving away of yourself to another. Christ said, "I have told you this so that my joy may be in you and that your joy may be complete. My command is this: Love each other as I have loved you. Greater love has no one than this, that he lay down his life for his friends" (John 15:11–13 NIV). We must, no matter how difficult it may be, take our faith principles (love) into our marriages, or we are not understanding the overwhelming effect Christ has on every aspect of life. Strive for Christian perfection in all you do, even in your marriage.

God of love who brings joy to life, may we today recommit ourselves to your concept of marriage, love, and life itself. May the way we strive toward your ideals, in every aspect of life, be a witness to others of the reality and value of being a Christ follower. Please bring understanding and peace to our world, which is in such chaos. Encourage us to find solutions to challenges, togetherness to strife, and be unity seekers in a divided world. May your love prevail in our marriages, our churches, and our world in general. Amen.

The Impossible Solution—Unless

There is a difference between peaceful protests and destructive and hateful rioting. Peaceful protests are justified when people see an out-of-control protector of the people using unnecessary force to subdue a suspect, causing the death of that suspect. Destructive rioting destroys the message of human outrage by becoming the focus of fear and hatred. So how does a minister of the good news of Jesus's love for all people respond? How do I say something that will bring God's Word to light in the darkness of life's situation? I thought about just leaving the rest blank and ending by saying, "You tell me!" Yet the silence of Christianity has for too long allowed others to hijack the true message of God's Word.

I believe a message can always be found for times like these in God's Word. In Luke 10:25–37, we find the parable of the Good Samaritan. You know the story. A man was beaten by robbers. A priest, then a Levite, passed by on the other side. They did not want to get involved. Then a Samaritan came and took care of the man with compassion and love for someone who most likely would not have spoken to him in social circles. Jesus confronts us all with these words: "Which of these three do you think was a neighbor to the man who fell into the hands of robbers? … Go and do likewise" (Luke 10:36 NIV).

Let me say I am not a Samaritan—a person born of impure blood whose ancestors betrayed Judaism and worshiped falsely on the wrong mountain. But I want to be like the Samaritan who demonstrated compassion and love for someone he did not know. I would love for Jesus to use me as an example of what true godly compassion is all about. Wait a minute. Can you imagine what the people would have said at church on the Sabbath? Can you believe this supposed rabbi would use an illustration of the Good Samaritan and criticize our religious leaders? The message would have been lost.

Let me say I am not of African American descent. I do not know what it would have been like to have had ancestors who were slaves in America. I do not know what it would be like to hear family stories of cross burnings in yards or churches bombed. I do know this, however: while sitting in a McDonald's on Highway 80 in Jackson, Mississippi, with one of my best friends and roommates on a road trip to play Mississippi College, I began to feel what his life was like. It was in the early 1970s when I was in college and playing football for Samford University. My friend, an African American, and I were approached by the manager of the restaurant and asked to leave. I challenged his request. "Why?" His words have haunted me since that day. "I cannot afford to have a white man and a black man seen together in my business. They will shut me down." I know this was a different time and a different place, but is it?

I have said for years we never solved the racial differences in our country; we have just allowed the strife to go underground. Now we are seeing it resurface in full force. So what shall we do? First, stand on your Christian principles of love and peace. Do not allow your lack of understanding cause you to be hateful toward anyone. Second, take the time to get to know someone of a different race. It is amazing the things you can learn. Third, honor all policemen who are doing their jobs correctly. The vast majority do a marvelous job in very difficult circumstances. Fourth, be sure you isolate your distasteful remarks for those who are destructive and rioting out of control. Never allow a small minority to cause you to judge an entire group of people. Finally, act like a Christian, talk like a Christian, love like a Christian, and above all, be a Christian!

Creator of all people, enable us to face these challenging days seeking your plan and loving all people. Do not allow our hearts to be filled with hate. Let us as your people find solutions and not make things worse. Most of all, show us how during times like these we can shine the truth of your grace brighter than at any other time, because the darkness of this world is overwhelming. We need your light. Amen.

Trust God: Hope, Joy, and Peace

"May the God of hope fill you with all joy and peace as you trust in him, so that you may overflow with hope by the power of the Holy Spirit" (Romans 15:13 NIV).

These thirty-one words remind us about the grace of God and the affect that grace has on us. Allow me to put it in a different way. We believe in a God who brings to us hope. That hope fills us with joy and peace. All one must do is trust him. When we do trust him, the Holy Spirit causes us to be so full of hope that it spills out all around us.

Have you experienced this kind of faith? A faith that is so trusting of God that your hope overflows? I believe I have. I, however, must also say there are times when we are tested by life events causing anxiety that attempts to take over and overwhelm us. That is when we struggle to regain the feeling of absolute hope. Do you know what I mean?

This has been a challenging two weeks in our lives. Much of my time is spent each day trying to reinvent ministry without being able to worship at church. It is a process of retraining myself, after forty-six years in ministry, to do things differently. Things like writing a daily devotion. Then there have been people to call, people to encourage, and other challenges that go along with life and ministry. Challenging, yes, but fulfilling.

On Sunday afternoon we received a call from our daughter, Brook, telling us that our three-year-old grandson, James, was sick, and they were on the way to the doctor. After a quick exam, they were told his ears were inflamed. So the doctor prescribed antibiotics and said to check back in two days if he was not better. You know the routine.

The routine was shattered on the follow-up visit when the doctor said the antibiotics were not working and James needed a lung x-ray. If the x-ray showed pneumonia, he would have to be tested for the COVID-19 virus. She did say, "This is only a precaution." How do you tell yourself it is just a precaution when the x-ray showed pneumonia and they do test him for a new virus? What this means is we found ourselves praying that our James just had pneumonia. Strange, isn't it?

We are all quarantined until we get word from the test. The Woodwards at their home and Becky and me in ours. It really brings home how scary and emotionally disruptive this situation is for so many people today. In a heartbeat, an entire family's lives are altered.

I came across the above passage in Romans today, and it jarred me back into a spiritual reality. Trust God! Be filled with hope! Feel his joy and peace! Whatever the COVID-19 virus test says, I choose to be overflowing with the hope of God that brings us peace and allows us joy in the midst of anxious moments.

Healing Helper, give us faith even when our faith is tested. May we trust you for overflowing hope by the power of your Holy presence. Amen.

What Is Your Plan?

"There came a man who was sent from God; his name was John. He came as a witness to testify concerning that light, so that through him all men might believe. He himself was not the light; he came only as a witness to the light" (John 1:6–8 NIV).

I have always heard, "Make a plan, and work your plan." I personally came to the conclusion some time back that there is not a problem or situation that cannot be solved if you can see the desired result and begin to work backward. This way you can strategize step by step how to arrive at the desired solution. This is true with building a building and overcoming challenges of our world today. When there is no plan, the chances of success are minimal at best.

God always has a plan (Jeremiah 29:11 NIV). God always works out his plan through Jesus and through us. God is working out his plan today in the midst of this COVID-19 pandemic. Remember, however, he allows us to choose to participate or not. If we choose not to become involved, he will allow others to work out his plan. Will you sit back and be filled with doubt and fear, or will you join in with what God is doing?

God always prepares the way (John 1:6–8 NIV). Like John the Baptist prepared the way for the coming of Jesus, God has prepared us for a time just like this. I will admit I might be flawed in how I look at life. Yet it is how I have learned to cope and exercise faith. To me, everything that has happened in my life, my family, and my ministry brings me to this very day. God has prepared me for this time. Has he prepared you? I think yes!

God works through people (Acts 9:10–19 NIV). I believe in angels. The Greek interpretation of the word *angelos* is messenger. I believe God's heavenly angels are truly messengers to assist us in life. Our angelic concepts should not stop there. God's angels (messengers) are also people we know who say just the right thing to guide us toward God. Just like John the Baptist, as God's angel (messenger), guided people back to God. God will and does use his people to be his messengers today. Will you be one?

God asks for our insightfulness and ability to understand his ways (John 1:15–18 NIV). Have you ever played the what-if game? What if John the Baptist had not come first? Would people have followed Jesus as they did? It is not a matter of *if* God sent John the Baptist. It was his plan. We need to choose to accept God's plan, God's timing, and God's purpose. His plan works out much better than mine. Seek his plan and become a part of it.

God asks for our discernment (Mark 8:34–38 NIV). Wisdom is demonstrating a determination for being a part of God's plan in everything. I grow weary of people speaking as if they have an exclusive knowledge of God's will. They will often speak in words like "God told me to say (or do) this (or that)." I usually respond, "What if God has told me something different?" My limited understanding of God goes back to my call experience when I discovered the passage confronting me that said, "O ye of little faith" (Luke 12:28 KJV). I have believed it important to pray diligently then make a decision and get about accomplishing that choice. If you are wrong, admit it. If you are correct, give God praise for guiding you to his plan. But decide and see where God guides you.

Finally, choose to find God's plan in our situation! If you choose not to do your part, the picture is not complete. See the big picture and be a part of what God is leading us toward. The future is in God's hands.

Holy Spirit, help us to develop plans that are in line with the plans you have for us. Amen.

Leaning on the Everlasting Arms

How do you find peace in your life? There are many times that I retreat from the world and all of its troubles and—you thought I was going to say read my Bible and pray. That is a good solution. However, what I was going to say is I retreat into music. I will listen to classical music, which my mother introduced to my life. I will listen to classic rock, which carried me through my teen years. I will listen to country and Christian also. It all depends on my mood and where I am emotionally. This morning as I write this, I am listening to Bill Withers's "Lean on Me." "Sometimes in our lives we all have pain; We all have sorrow; But if we are wise; We know that there's always tomorrow."[8]

In my mind, almost every song has a message that can connect us back to God's Word if we let it.

David makes an interesting faith statement in difficult circumstances. His servants were confused that he was up and eating when his son had died. While his son was sick, David had fasted and wept. David's response was this: "While the child was still alive, I fasted and wept. I thought, 'Who knows? The Lord may be gracious to me and let the child live.' But now that he is dead, why should I fast? Can I bring him back again? I will go to him, but he will not return to me" (2 Samuel 12:21–23 NIV).

David had found peace during grief and sorrow, knowing God's promise. Maybe this was on his mind when David said, "The Lord is my

---

[8] Withers, Bill. "Lean on Me." Sussex Records, Inc. 1972.

shepherd, I shall not be in want. He makes me lie down in green pastures, he leads me beside quiet waters, he restores my soul" (Psalm 23:1–2 NIV).

David learned and, like us, learned the hard way to lean on God's loving arms. God throughout the scriptures has cried unto us to lean on him. As an example, Paul said, "May the God of hope fill you with all joy and peace as you trust in him, so that you may overflow with hope by the power of the Holy Spirit" (Romans 15:13 NIV).

We are going through unprecedented times in the world today. We need to find our peace, our hope, and our ability to trust, and that peace, hope, and trust is only found in Jesus who God sent so we could understand that we are not alone, even in a crisis.

> If there is a load you have to bear
> That you can't carry
> I'm right up the road
> I'll share your load
> If you just call me.[9]

Read God's Word; pray; find your peace in him who is always there for us to lean on in our weakness. When we do lean on God, we find true faith.

Holy One, hold us up in your strength today. Amen.

---

[9] Ibid.

Pray with Power

Do you recall the Garth Brooks's song from 1990 titled "Unanswered Prayers"?

> Sometimes I thank God for unanswered prayers
> Remember when you're talkin' to the man upstairs
> That just because he doesn't answer doesn't mean he don't care
> Some of God's greatest gifts are unanswered prayers …[10]

What do you do when you feel your prayers are unanswered? Begin to doubt? Start pouting? Pull away? We are human and are built with a sense of expectation of getting what we want. Maybe it is instilled in us when we are babies. We cry, and we get fed. We cry, and our diapers are changed. We throw a tantrum, and for peace, our parents give us what we want.

Is this the way we act toward God? Are we as a people of faith acting as if we cry and scream loudly enough, we will get what we want from God? Whine and whimper. Go ahead. My father would say, "Get over it."

When we mature, one of the great lessons we learn is how we are to accept responsibility and work for what we want. It is what we call growing up. It is unhealthy to remain in a childlike fashion. Paul shares some interesting insights applying this principle of growing up to our spiritual lives.

---

[10] "Unanswered Prayers" by Garth Brooks. Released on October 12, 1990, by Capital Nashville, a division of Capital EMI, Music, Inc. Produced by Allen Reynolds.

Brothers, I could not address you as spiritual but as worldly—mere infants in Christ. I gave you milk, not solid food, for you were not yet ready for it. Indeed, you are still not ready. (1 Corinthians 3:1–2 NIV)

So that your daily life may win the respect of outsiders and so that you will not be dependent on anybody. (1 Thessalonians 4:12 NIV)

We learn some great lessons from Paul for when doors are closed and we feel life is not what we want it to be. His missionary work had been halted, but then God opened a new world before him—Macedonia—the gospel went to Europe (Acts 16:6–10 NIV).

When you have a prayer that seems unanswered, when you do not seem to get your way with God, when all doors seem closed, when a pandemic/crisis closes the church, allow your prayers and thoughts to become something like this:

1. God, what are you trying to teach me and your church?
2. What new thing am I (we) willing to do for you?
3. What is God's plan for me and your church?
4. How can I (we) use this situation for God's purpose?

Spiritually open your minds, hearts, and souls to what God is wanting! Take the blinders off! Discover God's new direction for you and his church! He has a plan and a purpose! Let's dedicate ourselves to discovering it and joining him on this new journey!

God, I give myself and my worries over to you. Amen.

What Brings Fear into Your Life?

"But Joseph said to them, 'Don't be afraid. Am I in the place of God. You intended to harm me, but God intended it for good to accomplish what is now being done, the saving of many lives. So then, don't be afraid. I will provide for you and your children.' And he reassured them and spoke kindly to them" (Genesis 50:19–21 NIV).

Joseph's brothers were in fear that Joseph would treat them the way they had treated him. Instead, their fears were abated because Joseph realized he was where God wanted him to be, to do what God wanted done, in a time when it was most needed. When God is in our lives, our focus is different. Circumstances might not be easier, but we see God's plan rather than things that cause us fear.

What causes you fear? Horror movies, a desire not to fail, standing up in front of people, noises at night, or retribution from those you have wronged like Joseph's brothers? I think today the greatest fear is obviously the fear of what the unseen virus is doing in our world.

How does a Christ follower face fear of any type? How do we use faith to conquer fear?

Be honest with your emotions. Talk with your family and friends. Listen to them as much if not more than you talk to them.

Be faith filled. Allow God's Holy Spirit to calm you and trust God's divine will in all things.

Be a student. Learn everything you can about the subject you fear through reliable sources and conquer your fear through knowledge.

Be a trusting follower of Jesus. Believe God will use this situation to make us better Christians and better churches. He is opening doors for us if we are willing to walk through them.

Be a child of God. We lived in Birmingham, Alabama, during the civil rights era of the 1960s. Mother and Dad were out of town at a Southern Baptist Convention. In the months prior to their going out of town, Dad had worked diligently in trying to bring calm and encourage individuals to allow their businesses to desegregate. Due to his efforts, some individuals became angry and threatening. I received a phone call saying that they would never return alive from the convention. This caller knew where they were staying, the flight number, and the day of return. I called my father and told him what had happened. His response to calm me down was "Son, if they did not tell you their name, they do not have the guts to follow through." I know it was his effort to calm the panic in my heart, but it has always caused me to honor my father's advice. I want to bring calm and represent the peace of God we can all have through faith. As a child of God, we represent the highest power that brings peace, joy, comfort, calm, and assurance. Let's be like a child of God.

Jesus, continue to teach me how to be like you. I want to be a part of the family God has created. Our world needs calm, peace, and a freedom from anxiety. We know only you can do this. May we be your representatives in bringing this calm, peace, and freedom from anxiety by the way we live in faith. Amen.

Maintaining Our Faith When Faced with Restrictions

I read an article in the spring 2020 edition of the *Biblical Archaeology Review* titled "Brick by Brick" written by David Falk. It is a great article about how slaves in ancient Egypt made mud bricks and what the bricks were used for. He explained the workforce for the stone constructions, such as temples and pyramids, were Egyptian specialized workers. The Israelite slaves were building the homes for the Egyptian workers who were building their own places of honor and worship.

When Moses and Aaron went to Pharaoh to ask for the freedom of the Israelites, his response went to the heart of their pain. Pharaoh ordered the following: "You are no longer to supply the people with straw for making bricks; let them go and gather their own straw. But require them to make the same number of bricks as before; don't reduce the quota. They are lazy; that is why they are crying out, 'Let us go and sacrifice to our God.'" (Exodus 5:7–8 NIV)

When rereading the stories in Exodus, it struck me as to how the Israelite slaves in Exodus 5:7–8 were away from their homeland and their temple. The years away had caused them to lose faith and become withdrawn; they felt isolated from God. That is why God sent Moses. It was not just to free the slaves of Egypt; it was to bring his people back into a proper relationship with him.

In an attempt to slow the spread of the COVID virus, we now have laws that restrict our interaction with other people. We are isolated and socially distanced from our family of faith; we are unable to "attend God's house." Will we allow these temporary restrictions, no matter how long they last, cause us to fall away from our faith? By no means!

Our faith and connection with other Christians are not dependent on a physical structure. Our faith and connections are dependent on the ever presence of God wherever we are, whatever we do, whatever struggles or valleys we traverse. Remember the words of Paul who guided us through the early years after Jesus had finished his earthly ministry.

> I consider that our present sufferings are not worth comparing with the glory that will be revealed in us. (Romans 8:18 NIV) In the same way, the Spirit helps us in our weakness. We do not know what we ought to pray for, but the Spirit himself intercedes for us with groans that words cannot express. And he who searches our hearts knows the mind of the Spirit, because the Spirit intercedes for the saints in accordance with God's will. (Romans 8:26-27 NIV). And we know that in all things God works for the good of those who love him, who have been called according to his purpose. (Romans 8: 28 NIV)

Feel God's presence every moment of every day. Look for how God is actively using this time to bring about more than we can imagine or even envision if it were not for what is happening in our world today. Nothing hinders the Word of God, and nothing prevents God from being with us at all times. (See Acts 28:31.)

Sometimes it is so hard to trust you, Father, even though we know you are with us. Open our hearts to see your work daily, even in our times of crisis. May we learn from Moses's experience, though we feel unworthy. He trusted you. Amen.

Words: Doorways or Barriers (Part 1 of 5)

We usually think of words as doorways into understanding other people. Words can also become barriers because they can block people's understanding in what we are saying. In 1710 St. Paul's Cathedral's was completed in London. Queen Anne was said to have walked in and said, "It is awful; it is amusing; it is artificial!" What seems to be a criticism to us today was quite a compliment in her day. *Awful* meant awe inspiring. *Amusing* meant amazing. *Artificial* meant artistic. It certainly would not be easy to travel in a time machine, unless we studied what the words meant in that era.

Someone once gave me a new word that I have enjoyed from time to time. The word is *paraprosdokian*. Seeking out several sources, this word is a more modern use of the Greek. It is the combination of two Greek words: *para,* meaning against, and *prosdokian*, meaning expected. So the simplified version is "beyond what is expected." Allow me to try to express a sentence that is beyond the expected, starting one way and surprising you in the end. The best trip to Canada I ever took was to go fishing, but I woke up.

I guess that is why it is so important for us to say what we mean and mean what we say. The Bible puts it this way: "Let your yes be yes, and your no, no" (Matthew 5:37 NIV).

Turn in your Bibles to the psalms. Look particularly at Psalm 37:1–11. There are five words that I believe will open the doors into heaven and assist each of us to a better understanding of God's way for believers to live. Take these words and multiply by one hundred or even by one thousand when you add the New Testament discovery of God's grace through Jesus, and you will be in a totally different world reaching toward spirituality. Just see what I mean. This is where I want us to go for the next five devotions, a focused look at these five words. Today, I am going to look at *trust*.

"Trust in the LORD" (Psalm 37:3 NIV), David says. Then he refers to safe pasture. Trust God! Is it that simple? It should be! However, we live in a panicked society. If there is not enough to fear, there are plenty of others who will create more reasons to fear through conspiracy theories bombarding social media and on the twenty-four-hour news channels. There seems to be a diminished trust today with all in authority and even spillover into a lack of trust in God. So to trust God is a strange thing to do. The reference from David of safe pastures comes from his shepherding days. Sheep simply trusted the shepherd to find green pastures and still waters. They learned to trust because the shepherd was trustworthy. Jesus says he is the Good Shepherd. Trust him! What the world needs now is a willingness to follow the Good Shepherd. Let go of your anxiety, your fears, your anger, and feel his loving arms holding you up as you demonstrate your trust in him by giving him control.

Trust God enough to allow him to prove himself to you. He is more than trustworthy. This is the theory of the mustard seed, isn't it (Luke 13:19 NIV)? Just the faith of a mustard seed will grow into the largest of trees. That is the concept. Remember the old 1972 Alka-Seltzer commercial that said, "Try it. You will like it"? You, if you are like me, have tried a lot of ways to find peace, ease the pain of living, discover truth, and understand a better way. We seem to try everything else first, why not try *trusting* God. I do not mean putting the tip of your toe in the water type of trust. I mean, "OK, God, I will trust in you, your plan, your way, your timing, your love. I will trust you the way sheep trust their shepherd." What a new world will opened for you.

God of David and Father of Jesus, help me to trust you today and in the days ahead. Help me to understand your ways and your timing. Change my heart to be your love-filled heart. Amen.

Words: Doorways or Barriers (Part 2 of 5)

The previous devotion started a series related to words. I asked you to read Psalm 37:1–11. This is where we are returning today. The first word was *trust*. Trust God enough to allow him to prove himself to you. He is more than trustworthy. Today the word is *delight*. "Delight yourself in the Lord and he will give you the desires of your heart" (Psalm 37:4 NIV). Do you see the request and the expectation?

When I begin looking back at my childhood to see how I formed an opinion of religion, God, and church, there are two incidences that were most impressionable. Maybe this is part of why Paul wrote, "When I was a child, I talked like a child, I thought like a child, I reasoned like a child. When I became a man, I put childish ways behind me" (1 Corinthians 13:11 NIV). At least, I pray, I think more like a grownup today than I did then. The two situations both happened in church, or at least began there. Please remember I was not a child who would sit still in church. I was wiggling around, making noise with the hymnbook, then my dad, the preacher, stopped in the middle of his sermon and said, "I will continue when my wife gets control of my son." Mother immediately grabbed me, marched me out through the front exit, took me to the bathroom, and gave me a spanking. Then she said, "Don't you ever embarrass me that way again." I was being punished for being a kid. My interpretation: religion is something that gets you punished because you cannot sit still.

The second circumstance that affected my thoughts as a child was the Sunday that Mother sat next to me in church and said, "That's one. That's two. That's three." She went up to seven. Mother had a new approach. When we arrived home, she told me to go out to the tree in the backyard and pick seven switches. That's right. I had to get the seven switches. I was spanked with seven switches, seven times. That's not fair! My interpretation: God keeps a record of every wrong and will discipline us accordingly. Along the way, I learned to call that reasoning Old Testament theology. That is where one looks at the old covenant as "Thou Shalt Not." God as a Father, but more so a Judge.

What I discovered in the New Testament was a theology that was more of a covenant that said, "Love as I have loved you" (John 13:34 NIV) rather than a faith of not just restraining from things but doing things (James 2:18–19 NIV). Not religion out of obligation but a faith out of response to what we understand about God. Heaven and hell are real. God does judge. But we have an advocate who stands by our side on Judgment Day. His name is Jesus (1 John 2:1–2 NIV).

In other words, there is an entire attitudinal change between the Old Testament and the New Testament. Even Jesus would say, "You have heard it said, but I say unto you" (Matthew 5:21 NIV). So for me, Psalm 37:4 is a foreshadow of what is coming in the future. It is the ability to *delight* in the Lord. David says the delight comes from what God gives us. What more do we need than the forgiveness of our sins and the gift of eternal life? The Old Testament does spend a great deal of time talking about praising the Lord with singing, dancing, and music of all kinds. Yet here it seems to be more than just praising him for what he has done. It seems to venture into the realm of *delighting* in what he will do also.

Now let's string these first two words together: *trust* and *delight*. When we surrender our trust over to God, not waiting on him to prove himself, he will prove worthy of that mustard seed trust (Matthew 17:20 NIV). This developing trust will grow more and more through life. You will see him as a loving Savior, not just a punishing Judge. This is where *delight* comes in. Our *delight* in what we discover in God becomes an internal "living water welling up" within (John 4:13–14 NIV), and people will see in us our *delight* in him because of our joy in life. Two life-changing words that change our lives and can change the world.

God of mercy, we trust you and delight in your love. Let it show through us today. Amen.

Words: Doorways or Barriers (Part 3 of 5)

In the previous two devotions, we talked about *trust*, which leads us to the only true trustworthy One. We then talked about how *trust* leads to pure *delight* in the Lord as he blesses us. Today the word we will focus on is "Commit your way to the Lord; trust in him and he will do this" (Psalm 37:5 NIV). The word today is *commit*. It is so difficult to be committed to anything. We like to keep our options open. We do not want to be tied down or limited.

One might say in Alabama a person must choose where their commitments are. Take football. Either you are for Alabama or you are for Auburn. That seems to be an easy commitment. I grew up an avid Auburn fan. I received a recruitment letter from Alabama and did not even send it back in. I was an Auburn fan. My senior year in high school, I was a recruiting guest at every Auburn home game. To top it off, nothing gave me more joy than sitting with a close friend, who was an Alabama fan, while watching the December 2, 1972, Iron Bowl when Bill Newton blocked two punts, both picked up by David Langner and both run back for touchdowns. Auburn won 17–16. However, I vacillated in the late 1970s during some difficult years. I simply became a Samford fan; that's where I attended and played football. It made it simpler and more ministerial. Later, I became an Alabama fan because my children had become Alabama fans. Well, most of you would say, "Buddy, that is not true commitment. You should stick to one or the other." You are correct!

To *commit* is, according to Merriam-Webster's dictionary, "to carry through to completion." To commit is not riding the waves of emotions

    William P. (Buddy) Nelson

with your favorite teams; it is not being caught up in temporary issues of politics; it is to devote your life to that which you will see through until completion.

Wherever you stand on the racial spectrum, watching some of the memorials for Senator John Lewis, seeing his casket being drawn over the Edmund Pettis Bridge, seeing his body lying in state in the capital, knowing I had lived through those years, I had to say within my heart that is a person who made a commitment. All his life with all his efforts and all his energy, no matter what he faced, he was committed. What are we committed to, and how deep is that commitment?

How many churches do we see closing? How many churches are facing troubles? How many Christians seem to misplace their faithfulness in the midst of troubled waters? How many times has God asked us to take a stand and we wiggle out of committing? When we *trust* God, with that mustard seed of faith, we will discover the *delight* of his blessings. Then we have to follow through with *committing* to him. How can we not commit? If we trust, if we understand his blessings, if we are moving in a direction of faith and have come this close to God, *commit* all you understand about yourself to everything you understand about God and feel the peaceful bliss of being comforted in his loving arms. Look back the beginning of Psalm 37. Remember I asked you to read all eleven verses. "Do not fret because of evil men or be envious of those who do wrong; for like the grass they will soon wither, like green plants they will soon die away" (Psalm 37:1–2 NIV). This entire psalm's plan is to remind us that God is in control. Trust him and his timing. If we are to *commit* to anything at all in our lives, do you not think that commitment should be to the One who created us, loves us, forgives us, and is the only one worthy of our *trust*, the only thing we are able to consistently *delight* in? *Please, please, please* commit your life today to a deeper relationship with Christ! Find the true meaning of life-changing experience!

God, we trust you, and we delight in your blessings. May we all today, without reservation, commit to you and you alone. Amen.

Words: Doorways or Barriers (Part 4 of 5)

L et me remind us where we have traveled so far in our journey of discovery through words. We are looking at Psalm 37:1–11. We began with *trust*. Trusting God leads to pure *delight* due to his blessings. The third step in this walk of faith is once we have chosen to trust God and discovered the delight or joy of his blessings, which follow our efforts to trust, we must then *commit* to him and the life he wants us to follow. As remarkable as these first parts of the journey are, they have simply set the stage for the next: realizing the reality of what we have always believed was the impossible. "Be still before the Lord and wait patiently for him; do not fret when men succeed in their ways, when they carry out their wicked schemes" (Psalm 37:7 NIV). The fourth word is *still*. Be still, and wait patiently. How comfortable are we with silence? How comfortable are we with developing patience?

When we lived in Hoover, many events took place at the Galleria. All the events were designed to bring people into the Galleria so they would shop. The biggest event each year was the lighting ceremony that launched the Christmas shopping season. The Galleria was so packed that parking and driving in and out seemed to be an all-day affair. By the time people got inside, they were stressed, but then they had to wait for it to begin. Talk about testing your patience. Wall-to-wall standing people.

One year, when my father was in his eighties and getting very feeble, he decided he wanted to attend. Becky worked at Laura Ashley on the second floor with a view of the food court where all the action was to happen. The balcony was full, so we went into the store, moved a mannequin over to make room in the window, and there stood my father seeing what he wanted to see yet looking like a department store mannequin. The entire event has been etched into our thoughts as a wonderful time we had with Mother and Dad not long before his death. Normally, the process of securing a safe place for my dad would be too much trouble. I am so glad I listened to my heart rather than my impatience. Blocking out my anxiety, we were able to secure a place for my dad to watch the event he so wanted to see, and we accomplished what my father had asked of us.

If you *trust* God, if you *delight* in his blessings, if you have chosen to *commit* your life to him, be *still* and wait patiently on him. Calm down. Stop panicking. Do not be in a hurry. Do what our Heavenly Father asks, and experience his blessings in his time. We want the quick fix. Do you recall the commercial "I want my money, and I want it right *now*"? That is us with all the things in life we want. God's timetable is not our timetable. However, when we are calm and wait patiently for his timing, it is always better than what we expected. Is this not what the scripture means? "The Lord will fight for you; you need only to be still" (Exodus 14:14 NIV). "Be still, and know that I am God; I will be exalted among the nations, I will be exalted in the earth" (Psalm 46:10 NIV).

We are going through strange times. We are on a journey that we have never experienced before. There are no current guidebooks to show us the way. We are, as the old Westerns used to say, "shooting from the hip." We are either frozen in a panic, doing the best we can, or looking for what God has in store for us. Let's choose to be *still* and look for God. Never has there been a problem too big for God. Never has a crisis arisen in his world that God has not chosen to use to bring his people closer to him and enable them to do his work more purposefully. Be *still!* Be patient! *Trust, delight, commit,* and be *still* so you can hear God's voice of calming peace.

Father, enable us to show the patience, calm, peace, and stillness that only comes through faith in you. Amen.

Words: Doorways or Barriers (Part 5 of 5)

Today is our final look at Psalm 37:1–11. We have been looking at five words, their meaning, and how they are strung together to enable us to see the progression of the faith experience in a person of faith. We began where faith begins: trust. There can be no faith in God unless we first choose to trust him. Once we have exercised our inner ability to trust, there is a resulting delight. One cannot comprehend the blessings of God until trust is first in place. The blessings bring more than joy; it is pure delight in knowing what God has done, is doing, and will do in our lives. The snowball effect comes into play when trust leads to delight and then we cannot help but feel our hearts leading us to commit to God's ways. It is no longer an experiment. It becomes a life choice. We become his possession and are determined to be always on his side of all issues of life and even after life. When we completely commit, we then learn to be still, trusting becomes confidence. Confidence that God is in control. We trust not only in him but also his timing. In the stillness of faith, we feel his presence, which brings peace, calmness, and recognizing the Holy Spirit or, as I like to say, the holy presence of God. This leads us to the final word. It is found in verse 8. Refrain! "Refrain from anger and turn from wrath; do not fret—it leads only to evil" (Psalm 37:8 NIV).

There are three things that need to be addressed at this point. First is this concept of refraining from anger. Was not Jesus angry in the temple (John 2:14–15 NIV)? What about the Bible talking about God being angry (Romans 1:18 "Wrath of God")? Yes, there is a righteous anger when we fail to see God's way and when we are hurting the message of

God through utilizing the church or Christianity itself for false purposes. However, there are also places where we are taught to not let the sun set on our anger (Ephesians 4:26 NIV). And there are the many references of controlling anger as a part of faith (Romans 2:8; 2 Corinthians 12:20; Ephesians 4:31; Colossians 3:8; and 1 Timothy 2:8).

The second point to address here regards having a short-circuited faith. Go back to how these five words are strung together with a golden thread by the psalmist. Trust, delight, commit, be still, and then refrain. There is a question each of us needs to answer. Can you have the second without the first, the third without the second, the fourth without the third, or the refrain from anger without the others? The Good Shepherd is leading us to greener pastures and still waters (Psalm 23). Yet we need to take each step in following him to get where he wants us to go. Is this why there is so much confusion within the Christian faith? Is this the reason there is so much division within churches? Is this why we are not being effective in changing our world for Christ? I think so. We need to get back to better discipleship and being determined to grow Christians into the likeness of Christ.

The third point to address here is how Jesus and his teachings take the psalmist's teachings and pull them together with the golden thread of God's grace. I am not perfect. You are not perfect. We are, however, to run this race of life like Paul said by striving toward the goal (1 Corinthians 9:24) not just to the commit level but all the way to refrain from anger. The perfect example of fulfilling this was Jesus, who said, "Father forgive them" (Luke 23:34 NIV). He also said, "Love as I have loved you" (John 13:34). Then to tie the knot into the golden thread pulling these five words together, God's grace also gives to us the Holy Spirit to convict us, guide us, and empower us to accomplish more than we ever could by ourselves (John 4:15–16 NIV). The psalmist set out goals; Jesus says, "With my help you can do this" (Matthew 28:20; Philippians 4:13).

Heavenly Father, you gave us a step-by-step manual of what to do and how to do it. Encourage us to complete the task you have set before us with your Holy Spirit as our guide. Amen.

Are We Really Free?

"**I** want my own car!" "Why do you feel you need your own car?" "Because I am not free to do what I want to do, when I want to do it, as long as I have to share a car with my sister." That was a shortened version of a heated discussion I had with my father during my freshman year in college. My sister, Mary Grace, was a year ahead of me. We shared a car since we were both at Samford, and to my parents, it seemed practical. Why pay for two cars? To me as a freshman, it seemed ridiculous to have to ask permission to use the car. So here was the deal that was coordinated by my father. I should have had legal representation before agreeing. He said, "If you will work all summer and save up your money, I will pay half of whatever car you can afford by the fall." Deal! What have I done? The job was my first summer to work at the steel mills in Fairfield, Alabama. So many stories from working there, so many lessons. The first thing I learned was if you work one double shift, you make good money; if you work two double shifts, you work for the government. You must work either one or three double shifts to make extra money. Another thing I learned was if you doubled over on a holiday, you get time and a half for the first shift and double time and a quarter for the second shift. I volunteered for every double shift I could and even worked a straight twenty-four hours once. I averaged way too many hours working second and third shifts. I wanted my own car. I wanted my freedom. By fall I had enough to pay for my half of a car. Dad paid the other half. I had my freedom. Then the next conversation began when I said, "I need a little more monthly income to pay for gas." "Nope. You bought your car; you have your freedom; now it is time for you to learn about the responsibility that goes along with freedom. You pay your gas, service, and by the way, the insurance too."

What? As frustrated as I was then, now as I look back, I realized this was the best lesson for me. It taught me responsibility and a work ethic that has guided me in life and faith.

When we study the idea of freedom in God's Word, we find a multitude of references. Freedom to eat of all the trees in the garden except one (Genesis 2:16–17 NIV). Freedom with responsibility. Then Jesus talks about really learning about Jesus's teachings—and the truth will make you free. Freedom with responsibility (John 8:32–36). Then look at 1 Corinthians 10:23–11:1. Paul talks about meat that was sacrificed to idols and whether or not Christians should participate. He says three vitally important things that apply. "Everything is permissible, but not everything is beneficial" (1 Corinthians 10:23). "So whether you eat or drink or whatever you do, do it all for the glory of God. Do not cause anyone to stumble, whether Jews, Greeks or the church of God—even as I try to please everybody in every way. For I am not seeking my own good but the good of many, so that they may be saved" (Corinthians 10:31–33 NIV). There it is again, freedom with responsibility.

God gives us freedom to live in his world, yet he also gives us the responsibility to care for it and to be responsible. God gives us a new kind of freedom in Christ, yet it is a freedom to serve him. In America, we are given freedom to live in a democracy and freedom to find work, buy cars, and do many things, but that freedom comes with responsibility. My freedom stops at the line drawn where another person's freedom begins. As a Christian, we are free to do many things, yet we are responsible for how what we do affects another person. Here is Paul again speaking to freedom and responsibility: "For I am not seeking my own good but the good of many, so that they may be saved" (1 Corinthians 10:33 NIV). "Follow my example, as I follow the example of Christ" (1 Corinthians 11:1 NIV).

I am glad my father taught me the difficult lesson of responsibility that goes along with freedom. It helps me understand God's teachings.

Father, teach us to respect others more than we want for ourselves. We are free as your people and as Americans, yet freedom comes with responsibility. May we be responsibly free. Amen.

Being Boldly Faithful in Difficult Circumstances—How?

In spring 1978, I had been a full-time pastor for less than a year when the call arrived. It was a Saturday afternoon, and the call came from Baptist Medical Center Montclair. My father's heart bypass surgery had been a couple of days before, so I was alarmed when the nurse said, "Please hold. Your father wants to talk to you." The first indication that something was wrong was hearing his voice. It was breaking up, obvious tears and emotion coming from the man I had never seen cry or show that kind of emotion. This stoic gentleman was like a child who was in trouble. When I asked what was happening, he simply said, "Please get someone to preach for you. I need you here *now!*" In a panic, I knew I needed to go. I had a wedding later that evening so I asked a friend to perform the wedding for me. I worked other details out and left. I drove way too fast. When I arrived in the cardiac stepdown unit, I walked into his room, and he began to tell me the story. "Buddy, I want you to know that something happened during surgery. I do not know what it was, but I will never be afraid of death again." Then came an outburst of pure, unrestrained emotion, tears, and what seemed like a smile amid it all. I knew I needed him to calm down. I said, "Dad, let's finish this conversation in the morning." He agreed and went to sleep in a few minutes. I sat with him all night. I did not sleep, yet he slept like a baby. The next morning, I asked if he wanted to finish his story. He did not remember the experience or the conversation. I will always regret not letting him finish the conversation that Saturday night. However, let me say this: The doctor had told us he had almost lost my father on the surgery table during the heart bypass surgery. Also, Dad was obviously never anxious about death or dying the rest of his life. Even when he was in a nursing home for his last ten days due to dementia, he simply spent his time singing the great hymns of faith he had learned throughout his life. He left for heaven in peace almost twenty years after that heart surgery, singing with joy.

When we live in this world, we face challenges, changes, and constant distractions. It is so easy to become consumed with what's wrong and who is to blame. It is so easy to be distracted in difficult circumstances. Look at Paul, my New Testament hero. He was a real person who lived a real life and came to know Jesus after Jesus's earthly ministry. It was that Damascus road experience (Acts 9:1–19 NIV) that caused Paul to realize the resurrection was real and personal. It changed Paul's life forever. When you read through the book of Acts, you will encounter the difficult circumstances Paul faced. Challenges from the religious right in Judaism who wanted to shut him up, challenges from Rome for stirring up trouble, challenges from churches because he was trying to teach the churches to be true to Christ's principles. All this does not include snakebites, shipwrecks, trials, prison, etc. Yet we read a statement that seems to summarize Paul's life. "For two whole years Paul stayed there in his own rented house and welcomed all who came to see him. *Boldly and without hindrance* he preached the kingdom of God and taught about the Lord Jesus Christ" (Acts 28:30–31 NIV). Boldly and without hindrance he kept on going. Why? He knew without a doubt Jesus Christ was resurrected. Because of this, he had no fear for what was to happen to him in this life or the next. He knew the resurrected Christ.

That's the point of my private family story of my dad after surgery. Something happened that night! He had believed in Christ, preached Christ, and lived Christ for many years. But after that night, in his words, "I will never be afraid of death again!" Life changed. His and mine.

This world may not be what you want it to be. The situations of sickness and divisiveness are extremely stressful. We need, more than ever before, to live like we believe and are absolutely assured of the resurrection. That is what the world needs to see. Christians living so lovingly, confidently, and boldly faithful that they will want to have what we have. "Never to be afraid of death again!" Life changing.

> Confidently we come before you, our Creator, asking that we might be a part of your plan, not creating more problems. The world has enough issues. Let us, through our boldness of faith, change the world like the early Christians did, being boldly faithful in difficult circumstances. Amen.

Tradition!

The Merriam-Webster Dictionary defines *tradition*[11] as "an inherited, established, or customary pattern of thought, action, or behavior." One person said that the fiddler in the 1971 version of *Fiddler on the Roof* was a metaphor for "survival in a life of uncertainty, precarious as a fiddler on a roof trying to scratch out a pleasant simple tune without breaking his neck." We have, are, and always will be living in a time of uncertainty. The one constant in the lives of Christ followers is our faith. The belief that God is in control. The belief that God, through his grace, will one day raise us out of this world of uncertainty and allow us the honor of living eternally with him in glory.

Through all the history of Christianity, the church has struggled to identify itself and hold on to the traditions that have guided generations to where we are today. The early churches struggled because their traditions had been founded upon the old Jewish traditions. The Passover, the temple, the synagogues, the Torah, etc. Suddenly, they were thrust into a world where there was hostility, and the believers felt on the outside with no door to get back in. Paul's ministry was largely focused on keeping the teachings of the apostles true and accurate and helping churches to figure out what to do to be faithful.

In Paul's letter to the church at Colossae, he said, "Let the peace of Christ rule in your hearts, since as members of one body you were called to peace. And be thankful. Let the word of Christ dwell in you richly as you teach and admonish one another with all wisdom, and as you sing psalms, hymns and spiritual songs with gratitude in your hearts to God.

---

[11] "Tradition." *Merriam-Webster.com Dictionary*, Merriam-Webster, https://www.merriam-webster.com/dictionary/tradition. Accessed December 30, 2021.

And whatever you do, whether in word or deed, do it all in the name of the Lord Jesus, giving thanks to God the Father through him" (Colossians 3:15–17 NIV).

I grew up in a church that was more liturgical, or formal, than many Baptist churches. It was simply my experience in church. I have been to services in a variety of traditions: Catholic, Presbyterian, Methodist, Church of Christ, Church of God, and all kinds of Baptist churches. The experiences I have had have led me to the conclusion there is not just one way to worship or one way to be a church. I like what Paul said when he used the term "and whatever you do." Traditions connect us with our past, yet many times, they blind us from the future. The world is in constant change mode. We need to adapt to stay relevant. The message can never change, but the presentation, just like in Paul's day, must communicate to the people of the day.

I believe we as faithful witnesses should not be so caught up in our traditions. If so, we fail to see where God himself may be leading us in the future. There is only one outcome for the church if the average age of congregations continues to elevate. There must be an infusion of young families in all of our churches if there is to be a future. If we want to truly perpetuate the church, we must find new ways to reach those who may not be as comfortable with the older traditions. It takes a strong person of faith to place their selfish traditions behind them so there is an investment in the future of God's church. Maybe that is why Paul implies whatever you do, it should be about worshiping God with gratitude. Not just continuing old traditions.

God, keep us true to the faith and allow us to find the peace and assist your church in creative ways to accomplish your kingdom's work here on earth. Amen.

How Is the Wind Blowing in Your Life?

Just something to think about today. Did you know when you go sailing, it is not a matter of which way the wind blows? Sailing is determined by how you set your sail. I know very little about sailing, other than I have always wanted to go sailing on one of those big sailboats. I was captivated by the poem "Sea Fever" written by John Masefield in 1902.

> I must down to the seas again, to the lonely sea and the sky,
> And all I ask is a tall ship and a star to steer her by;
> And the wheel's kick and the wind's song and the white sail's shaking,
> And a grey mist on the sea's face, and a grey dawn breaking.

Paul talks about being blown by the wind when he says, "Then we will no longer be infants, tossed back and forth by the waves, and blown here and there by every wind of teaching" (Ephesians 4:14 NIV). My interpretation is for us faith sailors to set our sails, not to be tossed around by the storms of life. We are to use the force of the winds to get to where we are traveling. We are traveling toward foundational knowledge and maturity, which brings stability and unity. Please understand when we want to be faith sailors, we set our sails with a purpose and a plan. We know what God wants us to do. This is true for individuals and for churches.

What kind of sails are you using today to set the direction you want your life to go as a faith sailor? You know, without sails, you are being tossed about hopelessly in the storms of life. There are three sails I want on my ship as I sail in the winds. They are found in these words: "Be joyful always; pray continually; give thanks in all circumstances, for this is God's will for you in Christ Jesus" (1 Thessalonians 5:16–18 NIV). Sailing through the winds of our world today, I want to have a sail of joy. I want to see the good things in life. I want to know the joy of walking with God. I want to know joy even amid sadness. It is who we have become when we walk with Christ. I want the sail of prayer. Prayer is the wind that blows, and "we do not know where it comes from" (John 3:8). Prayer catches the breath of God to carry us through troubled waters (Mark 4:35–40). Prayer is the assurance our joy is made complete through our constant connection with the Creator (Philippians 2:2). I want to sail with the sail of gratitude. I choose not to leave a wake of sadness, but my wake should be a wake of gratitude. I want people to know my life was joy filled, prayer filled, and filled with gratitude for all blessings that come my way. What sails will you set when the wind blows?

> Great Captain of the land and seas, may we choose the correct sails as we travel with you through life. The choice we make determines the attitude we live with. May our attitude be of a faith sailor with no fear of the winds. May we be able to get up and go out to face the challenges of today. Amen.

WILLIAM P. (Buddy) NELSON

The UNKNOWN StoRy of God's GRace

There are many untold stories of God's grace. Stories, if they were told, would shatter one's opinion of individuals who are now living a glorious life for our Lord. Stories that are kept deep within our hearts because we are afraid of how people would perceive them. Yet on the other hand, the stories would be marvelous testimonies of how God changes us when we seek him. Isaiah says, "Seek the Lord while he may be found; call on him while he is near. Let the wicked forsake his way and the evil man his thoughts. Let him turn to the Lord, and he will have mercy on him, and to our God, for he will freely pardon" (Isaiah 55:6–7 NIV).

I said on one occasion, "God places some interesting people in my life." In most situations, I am referring to challenging people who are resistant to committing their lives to Christ and joining his church. One example was a family that was more involved in the church than most members yet took nine years to join. Others I often refer to as interesting people are people who I have become great friends with, served as their pastor, and enjoyed working together in God's kingdom work. However, these interesting people have been guilty of crimes, such as murder, bank robbery, drug abuse, alcoholism, and adultery. There have also been good church individuals who have lived a lifestyle that would be inconsistent with what we learn from scriptures yet don't seem to see the inconsistency.

What I have learned from the interesting people God places into my life is threefold: First, I have seen how God's grace has touched their lives. I have been a part in a small way of seeing lives radically turned around and made complete. I have seen how truly one could say like Paul, "I am the worst of all sinners" (1 Timothy 1:15 NIV) yet be used by God. Second, I have unfortunately seen what "good Christian churchgoers" do with knowledge a person's life before Christ. They have used it against them, making sure the rumors of the past keep resurfacing as if God had given them the personal responsibility to make sure those thoughts were kept alive. God may forgive them, but I (we) will never forget. Third, through it all, I have learned, as one person, to move away from the judgment of the past and discovered the path of accepting a person, any person, where they are presently in life. I think when you put faith, hope, and love into a blender, what you will find as a result is what I think would be God's concept of grace and forgiveness. Accept a person, any person, where they are, not where they have been. Isn't that the backstory of the prodigal father (Luke 15:11 NIV)? Isn't that the story of Paul? (Acts 9)? Isn't that our story? It is mine.

"'For my thoughts are not your thoughts, neither are your ways my ways,' declares the Lord. 'As the heavens are higher than the earth, so are my ways higher than your ways and my thoughts than your thoughts'" (Isaiah 55:8–9 NIV). Yes, God thinks differently from how we do. Yes, his ways are different from our ways. Yet he implores, beseeches, begs, requests, appeals for us to follow in his ways. He asks us to love as he loved us. He asks that we forgive as he forgave us. Maybe it is time we quit using our humanity as an excuse and become more like the Savior who through God's grace provided a way to rise above earthly ways. We need to truly seek his ways while he may be found. When we find him, become like him.

> Gracious, loving God, thank you for the forgiveness you have given me so my life can become more like you. May I learn to accept all people where they are without holding their past against them. Let us all learn to be as gracious as you are to us. Amen.

FeaR oR PRaise: Choose

There is a stretch of interstate between Chattanooga and Knoxville, Tennessee, that will cause you to pause. *Do I really want to go forward?* The signage causes trepidation. One's internal alert system goes off when the lights are flashing. The sign says, "Extreme fog area. Proceed with caution." Then you see it coming at you like a desert dust storm. A wall of cloud so thick that you wonder if your car can drive around it to avoid going through it. Then reality sets in as you become totally engulfed in the fog. You cannot see the cars one hundred feet in front of you. Even eighteen-wheelers are pulling over to the side of the highway. Movies flash through your memories. Not the happy ones. Movies like *The Mist, The Fog,* and even *30 Days of Night.* None of which I recommend. It just demonstrates where our minds go when we are in fearful situations. When we cannot see where we are going, we always fear the worst. We just do not want to be in an uncomfortable situation in life, whether it is driving through fog or wondering what might be around the next corner in life. Here is a question for you: In life we have beautiful days and we have days of fog where we cannot see the future and feel fearful. Is your life in a fog? Do you really know what is ahead of you? We may know where we stand at any one moment in time. We may know where we have been. But can you honestly tell me that you can see through the fog of life into the future? There are roads to follow, signs to warn and direct us, and experiences that inform us that we have been here before. All these bring a sense of confidence and even some boldness, but "Proceed with caution" is always a good motto. Or is there another word we should use?

Wait for it!

Yes, it is fear.

In Psalm 57, we discover David hiding in a cave because of fear. Saul, the king who once needed him, now was after him. David ran away and hid. This psalm is so very beautiful not just for the words we read, but more so knowing David wrote it at the height of his fear of death, nowhere to run, thinking all was about over, the clouds of what's next were encompassing him, so he talked to God. Oh, to be able to talk with God the way David was able to do! Read the entirety of the psalm. Wow! Unbelievable! Words that began because of fear but words chosen to praise God! Look at the last three verses. "I will praise you, O Lord, among the nations; I will sing of you among the peoples. For great is your love, reaching to the heavens; your faithfulness reaches to the skies. Be exalted, O God, above the heavens; let your glory be over all the earth" (Psalm 53:9–11 NIV). David did not fear driving through the fog of life. He embraced it. He was able to embrace the unknown, for he was traveling with God.

Here it is. I asked you to wait for it. The second word—which is better than *caution*, overcomes fear, empowers us when in the fog of life, provides the ability to praise God, even when hiding in a cave from death—is *faith*. That's it, folks! Choose between fear and faith. Faith is the bridge to the future. Faith is the confidence to keep on living. Faith is the belief in how great God is. Faith is what allows us to stumble, fall, yet get back up and move to a better place in life. Faith is our light in darkness. Faith is our confidence that everything will work out when we trust God. Faith allows us to be positive in the midst of despair. Faith keeps us working toward good rather than fearing what evil might come.

It is a simple daily choice. Live in fear or live with faith. Everything looks different when the extreme fog zone is behind us. Faith is what gets you there.

> God of hope, give us the faith we need today to sing praises to you, even in the darkness of our caves of despair. May we today choose to walk with you in faith, knowing your plan is better than ours. Amen.

Finding What Has Been Lost

My mind wanders off in different directions, creating more questions than answers. On the way to preach one Sunday, Becky asked what was on my mind. That is her way of asking, "Do you feel strong enough to attend church for the first time since heart bypass surgery?"

My response was much more than she was asking. "I am just wondering, once again, how does one declare the truth in a way people will listen?" This is a real challenge in ministry and in life. It has been a challenge for me throughout my forty-eight years of ministry. Oh, it is so easy to dig down deep into your resource books or use thoughts from some other person to put together a string of pious platitudes that stir the heart strings of the masses. They respond with such favor that preaching becomes an addiction. Just tell everyone what they want to hear. Just use all the religious clichés and bring up the issues people want to hear, and people will say that was a great sermon. Sometimes, there is a need for the honest truth, even if people do not want to hear it. If ever we want to be God's children the way God wants us to be his children, we will need, at some point, to hear the unwanted truth.

Then in my conversation with Becky, on that drive to church, I transgressed into a study of history and how the Christian movement changed forever when Emperor Constantine, who moved the capital of the Roman Empire from Rome to Constantinople, had his vision prior to a grand battle in AD 312. He put crosses on his soldiers and they won the battle. Constantine baptized his troops as Christians. Christianity became a legal religion for the first time. Suddenly, with one vision and the winning of one battle, without a revival preacher or any personal decision made by the individual soldiers, a Christian army was created. Christianity and politics became permanently bonded into one.

The history of Christianity from that point forward has been more of a struggle to identify who's right and when are they right. The churches gained power with the collapse of the Roman Empire; thus, the Holy Roman Empire began in Europe. The church began to launch armies to defeat the Muslims in the Holy Land in the eleventh, twelfth, and thirteen centuries. Martin Luther said, "Enough is enough," and launched the Reformation with his ninety-six theses, made up of 339 words on two pieces of paper, nailed on the door of the Wittenberg Chapel door in 1517. America was founded on the principle of the separation of the church and state, based on the abuses of the state religion, mainly in colonial Virginia. On and on the story goes. What has been lost in the true New Testament church? What has been lost in the purity of Christ's teachings? The Gospel of John begins in chapter 1 with this: "In the beginning was the Word … the Word became flesh and made his dwelling among us" (John 1:1; 1:14 NIV). Then in the final chapter (21), Jesus, when he is restoring Peter, says, "Follow me … Feed my sheep" (John 21:15–19 NIV). "Go, and make disciples of all nations, baptizing them in the name of the Father and of the Son, and of the Holy Spirit, and teaching them to obey everything I have commanded you" (Matthew 28:19–20 NIV). What about Jesus? What about the New Testament church? What about the movement Christ launched to save the world?

I am just wondering, once again, how does one declare the truth in a way that people will listen? How do we find what has been lost? How do we know what is lost when we do not want to change our way of thinking? A quick suggestion: if you are still listening, let us turn our thought patterns totally upside down and see what happens. Instead of using a justification theology whereby we justify our attitudes and beliefs on what we want to believe, take the time to rediscover what has been lost in the purity of Christ's gospel, then judge everything by his standards. Discover, when we find what was lost, what Jesus might want us to see, to hear, and to live by when it comes to issues like a pandemic, racial issues, political deceptions, lifestyle, and attitudinal changes, and sit down and talk to people we are not talking to now. Start with where we got off the track of truth, then move forward with his truth.

God of constant love and forgiveness, nudge us to hear the truth of your Word. Amen.

Social Media and People of Faith

am sure I am venturing into an area that should be left to others. If you feel this is wrong for me to jump into the turbulent waters of social media, just stop reading and turn the page. In social media when most people read something they dislike, they will simply unfriend you. I hope this is not the case. Like it or not, social media is a part of our society today. As a part of our society, it actuality becomes a part of who we are. Social media guides public discussions, gives us access to facts, spreads false truths and gossip, and is a great tool for spreading the good news about Jesus. It is truly the best thing and the worst thing that has come into our lives, all wrapped up onto one convenient package. So how do people of faith deal with social media? One has to make a personal choice of what to read and what to send or copy!

"Do not merely listen to the word, and so deceive yourselves. Do what it says" (James 1:22 NIV). I suggest you read James 1:19–27 to get the full effect. Hearing is one thing. Doing is another. How does this apply to social media? Dr. Andy Tamplin was pastor of First Baptist Church of Birmingham in the 1970s when I accepted the call into ministry. He became an early and effective mentor for me as a young minister. He told the following story of a revival he preached in Florida where many Seminole Indians lived. One night in the small church the invitation was given, and a Seminole man came forward to accept Jesus as his Savior. He said, "I will be right back." The church watched and waited, then heard some noise outside. They turned to see this new convert to the Christian faith was walking with a few animals, belongings, and his family. He simply said, "You said when we believe in Jesus, we are to give everything to Jesus. Here is my everything!"

No one can tell the story the way Andy did, but this story, however told, is a parable in real life of what it is to be a person of faith.

I asked my father once why he believed so strongly about preaching on tithing. His answer was simple. The Bible teaches tithing is vital, and when you have a person's wallet committed to God, you have all of that person committed to God.

This brings us back to "Hear the word and do it." If we surrender our lives to follow Jesus, we are deciding to devote all we understand about ourselves to all we understand about God. We are deciding to devote our lives as Peter says. "But grow in the grace and knowledge of our Lord and Savior Jesus Christ" (2 Peter 3:18 NIV). We are determining to be "living sacrificing, holy and pleasing to God" (Romans 12:1 NIV). When we choose to follow Christ, we are choosing to "deny ourselves, take up our cross and follow Him" (Matthew 16:24 NIV). On and on we could go with all of the multiplicity of ways the Holy Scriptures tell us what we as believers are to do. In short, we are, in all we do, to please God, demonstrate our faith through the way we live, and never bring disrespect on the gospel we say we believe.

So why should what we write, read, and share on social media be any different? Why do companies use firms to search social media platforms to see what job applicants have said on social media before hiring them? How a person uses social media demonstrates their character and shows what kind of person they are. What do your social media comments and shares say about your faith? Make sure anything you place on your social media reflects Christ. If not, what are you doing? "Do not merely listen to the word, and so deceive yourselves. Do what it says" (James 1:22 NIV).

I say this one last thing about social media and faith. It has proven to be a great new tool to share the gospel, when used correctly. Just be careful. Everything you share and write reflects your message of faith.

God, thank you for the open door to share your truth through social media. May we use it wisely. Amen.

Should Have, Could Have, Would Have

The title of this devotion has been used in music, has been used to teach proper English usages, has been used to clarify excuses, and has been used in various ways with alterations. I was taught early in ministry that every preacher preaches four sermons on Sunday mornings: the one he prepared, the one he preached, the one people heard, and the one he wished he had preached. Basically, all variations are used to what was said and to clarify the confusion of the dissatisfaction of missed opportunities. I hope the words I just used helped you to see the confusion of the consequences of evaluating everything that has happened in your life. If the first sentence did not, the second should have. Words can clarify. Words can confuse. Words can enlighten.

"But the Lord God called to the man, 'Where are you?'" (Genesis 3:9 NIV). Words that pierced the heart of Adam because the words of God confronted him with his sin. "Then the LORD said to Cain, 'Where is your brother Abel?' 'I don't know,' he replied. 'Am I my brother's keeper?'" (Genesis 4:9 NIV). Words that crushed the wall of grief and guilt that Cain was hiding behind. They exposed him for who he was.

It has never been God's intent to cover our sins as if they never happened. It has never been his intent to simply excuse our sins away and just say it will be all right. That would be what physiologists would call enabling rather than confronting the reality of what is happening. A person who has problems with alcohol or drugs, a person who is living uncontrolled with a mental illness, a person who justifies sin and keeps on sinning, cannot continue in their crisis unless they have enablers who allow them to get away with problems rather than forcing them to deal with their issues. It is so much easier to say, "I should have, could have, or would have," than confront a person with consequences. Yet God sets out the standard for getting life correct. No coverup. No feeling sorry. He demands we admit we are sinners in need of a Savior who can and will forgive us if we confess and show sincere remorse. Is this not what the Bible teaches about salvation?

When you look into a mirror, what do you see? A sinner hiding from God? A sinner who is covering up their sin? Or are we seeing a person who's burden of sin is being lifted by Jesus. This is where the crisis of humanity is confronted by the pure grace of the divine. Allow these words from the Word speak to you today: "If we confess our sins, he is faithful and just and will forgive us our sins and purify us from all unrighteousness" (1 John 1:9 NIV). "This righteousness from God comes through faith in Jesus Christ to all who believe. There is no difference, for all have sinned and fall short of the glory of God, and are justified freely by his grace through the redemption that came by Christ Jesus" (Romans 3:22–24 NIV).

When you look into a mirror, what do you see? Be a person who has dealt with your sin and is no longer hiding. Be the person who confesses freely what God has done for you by forgiving you of your sins. Be a person who is no longer covering up their failures. Be a person who is joyously embracing the grace of God's forgiveness, proclaiming from the mountaintop, "Look at who I am today because I turned my life over to him, who sent his Son to forgive me. He can do the same for you."

Wait a minute! Is that where this is going? Is this the issue that confronts Christianity today? Are we becoming a faith of should have, could have, and would have rather than proudly proclaiming the truth of God's grace? What do you see in the mirror?

God of grace, may we serve you with boldness, honesty, and clarity. Amen.

PRide iN Defeat

It all began in the third grade. My weight was about 158 pounds. My parents thought it was time for me to learn to participate in afterschool sports. Because of my size, I played a lineman in football. It seemed easy at the time. The coach said to the fastest kid, "Get the ball and stay behind Nelson." I do not think I ever blocked anyone, but no one on the other team wanted to get in my way. We scored a lot of running touchdowns. Every year the challenges became more difficult and the competition became faster and stronger. Everything came down to the last game I would play in 1973. In all of those years, I never played on a losing team. Oh, we lost a few games here and there, but as for the seasons, every team I played on won more than we lost. Now the last game. We were tied with wins and losses. This final game would determine whether it was going to be a winning or a losing season. I wanted to win more than anything else. As time was running out, just seconds on the clock, we were ahead by just a few points. There it went, a long pass down the right side of the field. Touchdown! Game over! We lost! My first losing season through all the years.

I learned a great lesson that day. There is pride to be discovered even in defeat. We have heard so many times that winning is everything. It is not! Doing the very best you can with what you have is everything! When reviewing the film of that last game, I realized I had played the best game I had ever played. Finally, after fifteen years of organized sports, I had learned to give it everything I had to give. I played the best game, not compared to others but in comparison to my own efforts up to that point. My way of thinking changed that day. Do your best with what you have.

I think this is what Paul is talking about when he says, "Do your best to present yourself to God as one approved, a workman who does not need to be ashamed and who correctly handles the word of truth" (2 Timothy 2:15 NIV). "For I am already being poured out like a drink offering, and the time has come for my departure. I have fought the good fight, I have finished the race, I have kept the faith. Now there is in store for me the crown of righteousness, which the Lord, the righteous Judge, will award to me on that day—and not only to me, but also to all who have longed for his appearing" (2 Timothy 4:6–8 NIV). "I can do everything through him who gives me strength" (Philippians 4:13 NIV).

God does not expect us to be able to tithe equally, but he does expect us to do the best we can. God understands when we are not able to attend church every week, but he does expect us to do the best we can. God does not expect every Christian to be the best Sunday school teacher, but he does expect us to find our gift and do the best we can. God does not want us to compare ourselves to others, but he does expect us to strive for being the best example of Christ we can be.

Get it? It is not in winning or losing in life. It is finding ways to study, grow, and do the best we can, all the way up to the last game. It is being able to say, "I have fought a good fight, I have finished the race, I have kept the faith" (2 Timothy 4:7 NIV).

This is where the X marks the spot. Begin digging for the true treasure of life and faith. Do the very best you can with what you have, to be found faithful and obedient to God. This is where you will discover pride even in defeat. Doing your best!

Holy Spirit, give us motivation to do the best we can every day. Amen.

What Kind of Person Are You?

Which is more important: to ask yourself what kind of person you are or to ask other people what kind of person you are? To be healthy in mind and spirit, it is vitally important to look inward to see what kind of person you really are. If we do not seek deep within ourselves to discover all that makes us who we are, we are at risk of believing our unhealthy ways are normal. However, if we do some self-reflection adding to guidance with someone who will give us an honest evaluation, we can discover what it is to be healthy mentally, emotionally, and spiritually. So the answer to the question is we need to honestly look inwardly *and* we need to seek outside guidance to truly discover what kind of person we are. In simple terms, we need to clean out all the dust and dirt in our hearts to fully give Christ room so he can change us to become like him (Romans 15:7 NIV).

It is so easy to conceal our inner frustrations, fears, prejudices, and even block out horrid events from our past that affect us daily, even if we continue to cover them over with forgetfulness. It is as if we are holding a beach ball underwater. You can only hold that beach ball underwater for so long before it erupts back to the surface with an exponentially greater force. Why do I say these things today? If we want to be at our best in serving Christ effectively, we need to first know we are healthy in mind and spirit so that we are not tainting his truth, making it less than what it was intended to be. Paul says, "To be made new in the attitude of your minds" (Ephesians 4:23 NIV). And in the King James Version, it reads, "And be renewed in the spirit of your mind" (Ephesians 4:23 KJV). Additionally, Paul writes, "For by the grace given me I say to every one of you: Do not think of yourself more highly than you ought, but rather think of yourself with sober judgment, in accordance with the measure of faith God has given you" (Romans 12:3 NIV).

One of the most important events that is a part of our re-creation when we come to know Christ as Lord and Savior of our lives is when God says we are to change into the likeness of him. We are to love as he loved us. Something happens within us when we surrender to the change brought about by the faith we place in Jesus. We discover a new standard for living. Look at Philippians 4. This is a vital chapter if we want to know what kind of person we are and what kind of person we should be. Paul starts by saying we need to stand fast in the Lord. Then he goes into a beautiful description of a healthy Christian in verses 4–7. I see these verses as God's way of saying, until you arrive at this standard, you still have work to do. "Rejoice in the Lord always. I will say it again: Rejoice! Let your gentleness be evident to all. The Lord is near. Do not be anxious about anything, but in everything, by prayer and petition, with thanksgiving, present your requests to God. And the peace of God, which transcends all understanding, will guard your hearts and your minds in Christ Jesus" (Philippians 4:4–7 NIV). He then uses words telling us how to get to the standard that has been set before us. Words like whatever things are *true, noble, just, pure, lovely, good report, virtuous,* and *praiseworthy*" (Philippians 4:8 NIV). Words telling us how our minds should be working to arrive at God's standard.

Sound impossible? Then look at this thought by Paul: "I can do everything through him who gives me strength" (Philippians 4:13 NIV). And this: "And my God will meet all your needs according to his glorious riches in Christ Jesus" (Philippians 4:19 NIV).

What kind of person are you? Who we are affects how effective we are in sharing God's truth to the world. We need to be God's representatives doing God's work, God's way, in God's timing, in a world lost in sin. What kind of person will you become?

God of creation and re-creation, help us to live up to your standard so we can present your truth in a healthy way to change the world into a kingdom that is like yours in heaven. Amen.

Our Father which art in heaven, Hallowed be thy name. Thy kingdom come. Thy will be done in earth, as *it is* in heaven. (Matthew 6:9–10 KJV)

Printed in the United States
by Baker & Taylor Publisher Services